BRISTOL

Edited by Lynsey Hawkins

First published in Great Britain in 2003 by
YOUNG WRITERS
Remus House,
Coltsfoot Drive,
Peterborough, PE2 9JX
Telephone (01733) 890066

HB ISBN 1 84460 046 7
SB ISBN 1 84460 047 5

FOREWORD

Young Writers was established in 1991 as a foundation for promoting the reading and writing of poetry amongst children and young adults. Today it continues this quest and proceeds to nurture and guide the writing talents of today's youth.

From this year's competition Young Writers is proud to present a showcase of the best poetic talent from across the UK. Each hand-picked poem has been carefully chosen from over 66,000 'Hullabaloo!' entries to be published in this, our eleventh primary school series.

This year in particular we have been wholeheartedly impressed with the quality of entries received. The thought, effort, imagination and hard work put into each poem impressed us all and once again the task of editing was a difficult but enjoyable experience.

We hope you are as pleased as we are with the final selection and that you and your family will continue to be entertained with *Hullabaloo! Bristol* for many years to come.

CONTENTS

The Poems

WHEN I GROW UP

When I grow up I want to be
Something out of the ordinary
Not a builder, not a baker
Not a cook or undertaker.

When I grow up I want to be
Something out of the ordinary
A nurse, a vet, I'm not quite sure
A famous actress with a star on my door.

When I grow up I want to go
To different countries, like Mexico
And other foreign lands maybe
With shimmering shores and sparkling seas.

When I grow up I want to live
Somewhere that is expensive
A palace, castle or mansion will do
With gardens, lakes and a stunning view.

When I grow up I want to be
The very best that I can be
I'm not sure what, I'll wait and see
Right here, right now, I want to be
Me!

Katie Denton (10)
Colston's Lower School

NIGHT IN THE GARDEN

It's soft and peaceful
In a garden of France
The clear sky
Showing shooting stars
No sound of people
Just bats swooping

The darkness covers the fields
With cold, icy breath
No sound of cars
To disturb the darkness
Sound does not travel
With cold, icy breath

I look out of the window
The sun has not risen
I see all this
In a soft and peaceful
Garden in France.

Ross Denton (10)
Colston's Lower School

THE MAGNIFICENT DOG

My dog is as brown as a tree trunk
His bark is like a letter of the alphabet
His tail is like a crocodile's tail
His eyes are like twin sons
He resembles a tree trunk.

I will love my dog until he dies.

Dino Polyviou (9)
Colston's Lower School

The Falling Rainforests

Forests I see you tumbling,
In the dawn light,
One moment you are there,
The next you are gone.

We see people perishing you,
They don't care a bit,
Oh please forest stay, stay, stay,
We need you to exist.

Mountainous forests,
You are the king of plants,
You grow to extreme heights,
Don't let us ruin your life!

Tropical, boreal, coniferous,
We love you through and through,
Please will you forgive us,
Although we perish you!

Matthew Brock (11)
Colston's Lower School

Blue And White Day

Snowflakes are falling stars.
The trees are white, covered with snow.
Birds are mini planes, gliding through the sky.
The snow is pure ice cream.
The river is icy, wide and slippery.
Cars are skidding by.

David Jackson (10)
Colston's Lower School

My Magnificent Cat

My cat is black, as black as coal,
His purr is like a bee in the summer, buzzing,
His tail is like a feather, so soft!
His eyes are like two moons
Because they glow,
He resembles a pair of woolly slippers,
I will love him forever!

Nicole Mason (9)
Colston's Lower School

Blue And White Day

Massive snowflakes floating are paper aeroplanes.
The evil wind sprinting is a 100m runner.
Then an enormous winter tree thumps to the ground.
A little girl screaming to get away.
The howling wind gets faster.
Icy bodies sparkling and springing on high.

James Nicholas (9)
Colston's Lower School

The Magnificent Cat

My cat is ginger like a fox
Her purr is like a car engine
Her eyes are like fire
Her nose is like a pink flower
She resembles a cannon ball.

I will love her forever and ever.

Ben Fisher (9)
Colston's Lower School

SNAKES

Slimy slithery snakes all around
In the grass of the jungle
Even in trees, hanging from the branches
Hissing loudly, looking for food
Coiling around a tree
Tongues that look like little catapults
Shooting and darting in and out
They move very quietly
They are difficult to see
Because they are camouflaged.

Callum Wallis (8)
Colston's Lower School

BLUE AND WHITE DAY

The sun is as shining as a big orange beach ball
That always stays orange,
You can fish in clear blue water on a hot summer's day,
Waves are as high as a whale can jump when it gets angry,
Clouds are like cotton balls floating in the air.

Max Tarr (9)
Colston's Lower School

MY MAGNIFICENT CAT

My cat is ginger with a coat like a lion's mane,
His purr is like an engine ticking over,
His tail is like a soft belt,
His eyes are like meadow grass.

I will love my cat forever and ever.

Nathan Patten (8)
Colston's Lower School

Football Frenzy

'Rovers!' cried supporters up the road,
They were in a typical, loud, frenzy mode.

'City!' shouted the opposition,
To win against Rovers, was their mission.

The whistle blew, the game had begun,
It should have been a lot of fun.
In the first half, two goals were scored,
There was no chance, for the crowd to be bored.

There was a scuffle up in the stands,
The crowd's tempers were high,
A riot was at hand.

The police came in, in a bit of doubt,
How were they going to sort this out?

Finally the police were in control,
The public treated this like gold!

'Rovers!' cried the supporters up the road,
In a typical, loud, frenzy mode.

'City!' shouted the opposition,
To beat up Rovers was their mission.

Tom Pearce (10)
Colston's Lower School

The Snake

My snake is green like the grass
His eyes are like fires burning
His stripes are like the sunshine
His hiss is like air coming out of a tyre.

Andrew Bowen (9)
Colston's Lower School

The Magnificent Dog

My dog is black and white
Like a chess board,
His beard is like
An old man's beard,
His eyes are like
Black clouds,
His legs are like
A cheetah's legs.

He resembles a racing dog.

I will love him forever and ever
And ever and ever!

Greg Herbert (9)
Colston's Lower School

My Amazing Bedroom

My bedroom is big
And full of toys,
Radios, CDs and
Things for boys.

Blue sheets and duvet
On my bed
A star and planet mobile
Above my head.

I like my room
I love to sleep
And when I'm in bed
You won't hear a peep.

Harry Huish (8)
Colston's Lower School

Flying Over Colston's

I am flying, I am soaring, I feel excited!

The church spire is a giant's dagger,
The playing fields are his wife's patchwork quilt,
The children look like ants scurrying into an anthill,
The trees are flowers beginning to wilt.

I feel thrilled, I feel light,
The sun is wonderful and bright!

The sky is cold, red with anger,
The birds are flying beside me,
I can pick everything up in one big grab,
Even an old oak tree.

I feel thrilled, I feel light,
The sun is wonderful and bright!

My tummy starts to feel funny,
I'm going up and down like an
Uncontrollable bunny,
I'm falling . . .

Briony Brockhurst (9)
Colston's Lower School

The Magnificent Fish

My fish is silver like a shiny spoon,
His tail is like a triangle on its side,
His body is like sparkling water,
His eyes are like brown buttons.

Jamie Walsh (8)
Colston's Lower School

FLYING OVER COLSTON'S

I'm soaring over the big blue snake
Admiring its shiny blue scales.

I'm soaring over the little ants,
Playing in the big, green field,
I'm watching them scuttle here and there
Playing a game of football.

I'm soaring, I'm flying, it's really exciting
To admire the school,
From a bird's eye view.

I'm soaring over a patchwork quilt,
Which my mum has made for me.

Then I hear Dad calling me,
To come back home for tea.

Now that I am a bird
I hope it's not worms for tea!

Kathryn Parker (9)
Colston's Lower School

THE LONELY DRAGON

The lonely dragon, fast and strong,
His scales are like the colours of the rainbow,
He really was a magnificent sight.

The other dragons laughed at him because they were different.

The lonely dragon liked to breathe fire
To make his scales glow brighter.

James Wilson (7)
Colston's Lower School

Flying Over Colston's

Flying over Colston's
Soaring through the air,
Flying over Colston's
With no care.

Flying over Colston's
Seeing my friends have fun,
Flying over Colston's
I wish I was one.

Flying through the air,
The feeling's great,
Flying through the air
There's nothing to hate.

Seeing the children
Down on the ground,
Hearing them shout
And the laughing sound.

I see all the juniors
Going to class,
Some are late
And running there fast.

Instead of being there
Like I should,
I'm up here
Where the feeling's good.

I'm floating and flying
Through the air,
The feeling's better
When the wind goes through your hair.

When I come down into land,
My wings turn back into a hand.

Steven Ray (9)
Colston's Lower School

SUNNY POEM

By the blue sea there are rock pools,
Rock pools that are deep with red crabs,
Crabs walking through the salty water,
Water with little calm waves,
Waves making it fun for children,
Children burying their dads in hot sand,
Sand being dug up,
Up to the ice cream van for an ice cream,
Ice cream is lovely and cool,
Cool boats tied by the pier,
Pier under the hot sun,
Sun beating on the mums,
Mums asleep on the towels,
Towels wrapped around wet people,
People having a great time on the beach,
Beach lined with pebbles,
Pebbles shiny and smooth,
Smooth sand in-between toes.

Dan White (10)
Colston's Lower School

Frosty Days

Woke up this morning
It was freezing cold
My hands were numb
And my feet were cold
Like ice blocks
Put my gloves on
And went to school.

The tops of houses were covered in snow,
Like a fairy had sprinkled fairy dust over them
We waited in the playground
Freezing cold.

The bell went at last
And we hurried inside
The radiators were on
And we were all getting warm
Went downstairs
Past the cold air.

When it was break, nobody wanted to go outside
We put our warm coats on
And gloves and scarves and hats
Some people wanted to stand around
But they were soon as cold as the snow.

Home time at last
It seemed a long day today
I don't know why
Maybe it's because it was cold
And the breaks seemed long.

We are home in my warm house now
I went outside and saw the pond had frozen over
We got the fire going with twigs and sticks
The flames were like red monsters warming us.

Annie Krawiec (9)
Colston's Lower School

THE BEACH

The pier is packed with children,
Children building sandcastles,
Sandcastles knocked down by wind,
Wind making big waves,
Waves frothy, bubbly and warm,
Warm in the rock pools with shrimps,
Shrimps hiding from children,
Children play in the sea,
Sea filled with boats,
Boats at the harbour,
Harbour filled with people,
People eating ice cream,
Ice cream chased by wasps,
Wasps hiding under people's parasols,
Parasols shielding the sun,
Sun beating on the sand,
Sand, soft and yellow,
Yellow shells twinkling from the sun in the blue sky,
Sky as deep as the ocean,
Ocean full of living things.

Harvey Maggs (9)
Colston's Lower School

I Am . . .

I am a nutty guy who likes dirt-surfing
I wonder if there are griffins
I hear the leaves as they fall to the ground
I see me on a dirt-surfer riding down a hill
I want to kick-flip on a skateboard
I am a nutty guy who likes dist-surfing.

I feel the wind in my face when I go down a half-pipe
I worry that the sun will crash into the earth
I am a nutty guy who likes dirt-surfing.

I understand that you are supposed to go to school
I say that I am going to go to Gloucester skiing
I dream that I will be a pro skater
I try to be good at scrambling
I hope to behave better in L3
I am a nutty guy who likes dirt-surfing.

Sam Ford (9)
Colston's Lower School

Blue And White Day

Snowflakes are falling stars,
The snow is frozen milk,
Walking through a cave,
There are icicles that look
Like frozen fingers.
They fall as sharp daggers
Into the snow on the icy cave floor.

Luke Bailey (10)
Colston's Lower School

THE POACHER

The flapping of bats' wings
In the still, winter night.

Then quiet again
Silver clouds roll
On the moonlit hill
A gentle breeze floats through
The dark wood

An owl hoots
Then quiet again

A distant train rattles, whistles, rattles.

Someone's footsteps
A crack
A squeal
And quiet again.

Francis Blagburn (10)
Colston's Lower School

THE RAINFOREST

Deep in the jungle
Where the animals roamed
The bulldozers lived
Destroying their homes
Trees crashing down from the sky to the ground
Making the most horrific sounds
Pythons, gorillas and chimpanzees,
Crying out for themselves and their fellow trees.

Esther Carter (10)
Colston's Lower School

A Secret Sight At Night

The clock has struck,
Are they asleep?
Out she comes,
The girl who creeps.

Silently downstairs she goes,
Twisting, twirling, no one knows,
Outside she goes with crunching feet,
On the frozen grass who does she meet?

There at last, the willow tree,
And a knotty, gnarly seat
For the girl who comes along,
With tiny pattering feet.

Under the tree, crystals hang glittering,
While on the pond the surface is silver with ripples,
Some people say they are like lamps flickering
And they will never know what is true.

Suddenly! Dawn is breaking,
The crystals turn to water,
The girl runs inside and up the stairs
And into her bed, she doesn't care.

Bethany Wood (10)
Colston's Lower School

Parody

Jack and Jill went to the shop
To fetch a drink of pop
Jack stood up and hit his head
And Jill laughed and could not stop.

Warren Abrahams (11)
Colston's Lower School

Things At The Seaside

Speedboats giving water ski rides,
Rides all around,
Around the shore donkey rides can be seen,
Seen in the distance are ferries,
Ferries go to the nearest ports,
Ports are busy,
Busy like on hot summer days,
Days pass quickly when you're at the beach,
Beach bathers lying on towels,
Towels wrapped around children,
Children making sandcastles,
Sandcastles being destroyed by the sea,
Sea green,
Green like seaweed,
Seaweed in rock pools,
Rock pools make homes for crabs,
Crabs scuttle,
Scuttle across the sand hot,
Hot like a summer's day.

Henry Lowrey (9)
Colston's Lower School

Parody

Oh the grand old Duke of Colston's
He had one thousand boys.
He marched them round the rugby field
Before the game began
And when they were winning, they were winning
And when they were losing, they were losing
And when the referee called for time,
The very last try was mine.

Christopher Maggs (10)
Colston's Lower School

I Have A Chick

I have a white chick
Called Mick
Who is feeling rather sick.

She has quite a sore eye,
But she still manages to fly.

We all love her,
But we don't want her to suffer,
So she has come into our house to stay.

Ben Pearce (8)
Colston's Lower School

The Magnificent Horse

My horse is brown like a tree trunk
His mane is like brown feathers,
His nose is like fuzzy felt,
His legs are like long bones,
He resembles a massive bear,
I will hug him and kiss him forever.

Toby Morris (8)
Colston's Lower School

Parody

George Porgie, pudding and pie,
Ate lots of food as well as a fly.
When the boys called round that day
George Porgie was buzzing away.

James Cloake (10)
Colston's Lower School

A Blue And White Day

The ground is like a soft, white, fluffy blanket
And the winter sky is turquoise-blue,
The tall thin trees are like snowmen standing to attention,
The grass is spiky and glistens like silver daggers in the sun,
The walls of the houses are cold and white like cubes of ice.

Oliver Philip (10)
Colston's Lower School

Australia

A ustralia is lovely and hot,
U p in the mountains or down on the beach,
S traight down to the beach,
T he sun is hot so on goes the suncream,
R ight then, I'll race you into the sea,
A lright, you win, look at that boat,
L ast one up the mountain -
I can see the 'Three Sisters'
A nd the bushfires are burning . . .

Alisha Braley (11)
Colston's Lower School

Blue And White Day

Snowflakes are falling as shooting stars,
Snow feels like white, silky milk,
Children playing everywhere,
Snowballs coming from every direction,
Frozen people's fingers everywhere you look.

Arun K Mali (10)
Colston's Lower School

Seashore

In the blue sea, feeling quite cold,
Cold ice creams refresh you from the scorching sand,
Sand is golden white with blue deckchairs,
Deckchairs being used by mothers to watch their children,
Children digging excitedly to see who reaches water first,
First you're getting a tan, then you're playing in the sea,
Sea crab being annoyed by the children trying to catch it,
It was the grey donkey who made the funny footprints,
Footprints can be strange in the sand and sea,
Sea is where the crabs live in peace,
Peace is always at the deserted beach with the sea,
Sea makes moats for sandcastles and cliffs,
Cliffs with big white faces like the white sand,
Sand has big parts called piers,
Piers are for boats on which to anchor,
Anchor carefully, because of the slippery seaweed,
Shore of the beach is like sinking sand,
White cliffs are like walls rising high.

David Huggins (9)
Colston's Lower School

My Cat

I have a cat called Bennie,
He's big and fat and sometimes smelly,
He is always looking for mice
And when he catches one,
It is not very nice!

Jamie Denton (8)
Colston's Lower School

SUMMER BEACH

Everyone comes to the beach in summer,
Summer is the time for the beach,
Beach has wonderful sparkling sand,
Sand glinting on the beach,
Beach is home to tumbling waves,
Waves which glimmer in the light,
Light which forces you to screw up your eyes,
Eyes which see the happy children in the sea,
Sea which crashes on the shoreline,
Shoreline rock pools overflow,
Flows of water rush down the sand,
Sand gets moved by the waves,
Waves bring in garbage from the sea onto the rocks,
Rocks fall off the cliffs onto the sand,
Sand gets made into sandcastles
Sandcastles get broken by the waves.

Josh Harris (10)
Colston's Lower School

SOUNDS

A snake slithers,
Big Foot strolls,
A horse gallops
And a creepy-crawly crawls.

A cat purrs,
A tiger roars,
A bird sings
And my dad snores!

Calvin Peters (8)
Colston's Lower School

Deserted House!

The clock strikes twelve,
All are asleep,
Then they come out,
So silent, they creep.

Things come out watching,
With blood-red eyes,
No one sees them,
Perhaps they are spies.

Ghosts are waking up,
The bats are too,
Some chains are rattling,
Are they scaring you?

But that's not all,
Some things are gliding,
Vampire bats
And most things hiding.

Skulls are rising,
From the floor,
Most things are making
For the door.

Shapes and shadows
Are all dancing,
Spinning around the room,
Most things are prancing.

Outside in the storm,
There is flashing lightning,
Some people think,
It is very frightening.

Outside is where,
Most of it starts,
With no lungs
And no hearts.

But as the sun is rising
And dawn is near,
Getting closer and closer,
They just disappear.

Sophie Baber (11)
Colston's Lower School

THE SEASHORE

Colourful sea, bright sand,
Sand is shining because of the sun,
Sun is shining very brightly,
Bright red bodies lying in the sun,
Sun is shining on the sea,
Sea is fun for everyone,
Everyone is laughing because it is fun,
Fun children are very happy,
Happy adults are sunbathing,
Sunbathing on the sand, see the tiny shells,
Shells are pretty, with lots of different colours,
Colours of blue with golden sand,
Sand is soft on your feet and on your body,
Bodies rolling in slimy seaweed,
Seaweed at the bottom of the rock pools,
Rock pools also full of sand,
Sandcastles are made with buckets,
Buckets can be filled with anything like seaweed,
Seaweed can be any colour, red, green or brown,
Brown chocolate ice cream drips from your cone.

Anna Davies (10)
Colston's Lower School

STOP THE DESTRUCTION

The rainforests were put on this Earth to stay,
Until us humans got in your way
We left you barren
And cut you down
Just to save McDonald's clown.
We cut your down just for farming,
Which the animals find rather alarming.
Instead of you we chose
Skateboards, rubbers, pencils and
Death.
Animals flee at the sight of destruction,
Leaving you all alone,
Until the men come round
And chop you down,
So, please stop the destruction,
Before it's too late
And all of the greenery,
Is erased from the Earth completely!

Duncan Windsor (10)
Colston's Lower School

NIGHT

I am the bat who travels the night sky
But the ghosts and ghouls are my friends
But alas they are only trees, moving from side to side.

The church tower is my home but to people it is not.
But when we glide through the night sky we are ghosts.
But I am not an ordinary bat
I am a vampire bat.

Matthew Bown (10)
Colston's Lower School

Sunshine Is Fun

Ambling donkeys walk across the beach
Beach shells in all different colours,
Colours of deckchairs and ice creams,
Ice creams surrounded by wasps,
Wasps fly around and sting people,
People playing with and making castles out of sand,
Sand tickling your feet,
Feet wiggling, toes playing in the sea,
Sea salty and warm, people swimming and paddling,
Paddling and lying in the sun,
Sun shining so brightly,
Bright colours of swimwear in pedaloes,
Pedaloes sail all around the cove,
Coves in the shelter, so they are warm,
Warm rock pools with crabs and fish,
Fish are everywhere in the sea.

Ruth Stringer (10)
Colston's Lower School

Fireworks

Fireworks, oh fireworks, whizzing through the sky,
Fireworks, oh fireworks, the way your bright sparks fly,
Fireworks, oh fireworks, you light up the dark night,
Fireworks, oh fireworks, your bangs give me a fright,
Fireworks, oh fireworks, you explode like dynamite,
Fireworks, oh fireworks, you glitter in the night,
Fireworks, oh fireworks, you're such a glorious sight,
Fireworks, oh fireworks, made for our delight.

William Philip (10)
Colston's Lower School

TRAPPED!

I look down at the world below,
Tall trees, high hedges,
Doesn't seem so high from up here,
I'm tangled up in an ivy tree,
Where no one will ever see me.

I used to be soaring high, roaming free,
But now I'm stuck in an ivy tree.

From high up here I can vividly see Colston's School,
I can hear the children's cry,
'He hits a six!'
It doesn't seem that exciting to me,
I see other birds roaming free,
None of them stop to help me.

Earlier today I perched on a tree,
Over Colston's again to see,
Ants scurrying and hurrying,
The church was like an ice cream cone,
I swooped in for a closer look,
What a long time it took.

I used to be soaring high,
Roaming free but now I'm stuck in an ivy tree.

I was taken by a gust of wind,
Into the large looming ivy tree,
I wish I was somewhere else,
Instead of in this tree,
Life has just ended for me.

Kerala Drew (10)
Colston's Lower School

THE RAINFOREST

Massive rainforest on the land,
Rainforest, I heard you
Grieving.

Great rainforest, screaming for your life,
Screaming for your species, I knew
How we would use
Your destruction.

Chairs for our visitors,
Land for our houses.

Great land mass on the land,
Rainforest, I heard you
Calling.

Birds' high notes, keening, soaring,
At their edge a tiny drum
Like a tree beat.

We would make you
Dumb.

In the ocean of the rainforest,
Tree, I heard you
Humming.

Humming to your kind,
We'll never let you be,
Instead of life we choose

Chairs for our visitors,
Land for our houses!

Matthew Narey (10)
Colston's Lower School

My Trip To Spain

This year for a summer holiday,
We thought we'd go to Spain,
In Grampa's old and rusty car
It really was a pain,
So off we went to Plymouth
And drove onto the ferry
And there I met a lonely lad,
He said his name was Terry.
I really liked the holiday
There wasn't any rain,
The weather was so very hot,
Up on top of the plain,
I really liked the holiday
We had a huge big tent,
But by the time we got
Back home, the pole in it was bent!

Alex Beaves (10)
Colston's Lower School

The Magnificent Cat

My cat is ginger,
Like Geri Halliwell's hair!
His purr is like
The water going down the drain!
His tail is like a snake
Round your neck,
His eyes are like gold coins,
He resembles a gold star,
Floating to space.
I will play with my cat
Till his life ends.

Letisha Gollop (9)
Colston's Lower School

Dear Snow

Dear Snow,

Has someone hurt you so badly that you are trying to
Track them down and in every country you search you
Leave behind you a powerful, sly and destructive blizzard?

Why do you treat us with your bitter cold hatred?
Why can't you be friends with us?

Why do you frighten timorous children with your harsh
Coldness and your raging snowstorms which
Destroy the cities we live in?

Please, will you be friends with us?

Georgette Keane (11)
Colston's Lower School

Poems

Poems are lines and words stuck together,
With popular titles such as 'Pets' and 'The Weather'
They ring and they chime and they join and they rhyme
And the rhyme is beating at a steadish time.

Poems can be jolly and sad all in one,
With misery that cried and joy that has shone,
They burn with their happiness and learn from their tears,
But nothing will go, it just lingers for years.

Poems can be made up, like this one right here,
With facts that have been imagined,
Such as cows don't drink beer,
They inform and they say and connect, but they may
Simply change their odd minds on the day.

Alice Carpenter (10)
Colston's Lower School

THE SILENT HUNTER

Creeping along the moonlit streets,
Approaching the shadowy clock tower,
A subtle nod to each creature she meets,
Midnight's gone, it's past the hour.

Pointed whiskers, tail in the air,
The wind is crisp and clean,
Birds freeze as she fixes her stare,
Her beautiful eyes they gleam.

Climbing the steps, the cat spots her prey,
An ageing starling all alone tonight,
She hasn't eaten a morsel all day,
Though tonight is her lucky night.

The surprise attack is nearly complete,
Pouncing she knocks the bird out,
Standing over the corpse she chews the meat,
A powerful feline without a doubt.

Rose Attu (10)
Colston's Lower School

I AM

I am a Malaysian kid who likes maths,
I wonder why one with a hundred noughts is called a googol?
I hear spooky noises in the night,
I see vampire bats turning into vampires,
I want to be invisible,
I am a Malaysian kid who likes maths.

I pretend to fight with guns,
I feel the pain when someone shoots me,
I touch the trigger and make the gun shoot,
I worry that an asteroid might hit Earth and all life would be gone,
I am a Malaysian kid who likes maths.

I understand that I do not know everything in maths,
I say that criminals should be put in jail,
I dream that some day I will be a footballer,
I try to do my best in sports,
I hope that the ozone layer does not all disappear,
I am a Malaysian kid who likes maths.

Peter Ratcliffe (10)
Colston's Lower School

THE BLITZ

The blitz began in '41
And ended in '44
During that time
London became, no more!

Germany sent out her aeroplanes,
To inflict upon our nation fair
Mass destruction and mayhem
Everywhere.

The sirens ring across the sky
And through the air, the bombers fly,
Down to the shelter,
Our way we make,
The bombs crash down
And the earth does quake.

The king and queen
Through all of this
Stuck by their nation true,
They came through all of this,
But really, could you?

Shaun Malone (11)
Colston's Lower School

I Am

I am a lazy boy who hates school,
I hear the stamping of the teachers' feet in the corridor,
I wonder if school will vanish,
I see the gate which is locked,
I am a lazy boy who hates school.

I am funny and good at schoolwork,
I wonder if tomorrow will be a nice day,
I hear people talking outside,
I see fish swimming in the pond,
I want a PlayStation.

I pretend to be a car racer,
I feel happy with my imaginary friend,
I touch an imaginary burger,
I worry about the future,
I pretend to be a car racer.

Rowan Henry (9)
Colston's Lower School

I Am

I am a sportsman who loves football,
I wonder if footballs can float,
I hear people shouting in the background,
I see a ball go into the net,
I want to score myself,
I am a sportsman who loves football.

I pretend to play for England,
I feel that I'll score,
I touch the sky as I score,
I worry the crowd doesn't like me,
I cry that I did not get a goal,
I am a sportsman who likes football.

I understand not all the crowd likes me,
I believe there should be no dirty tackles,
I dream of winning the cup,
I try to help the team,
I hope to play for England,
I am a sportsman who loves football.

Calum Hughes (10)
Colston's Lower School

I Am

I am a smart boy who is religious,
I wonder if the world will explode,
I hear a dragon roaring,
I see a knight fighting on black horses,
I want to become a doctor who cures the poor,
I am a smart boy who is religious.

I pretend to fight in an army,
I feel scared!
I touch my bed and get scared of bedbugs,
I worry that I'll forget to do my homework,
I am a smart boy who is religious.

I understand that I should be sensible,
I say there should not be racist incidents.

I dream that I will live in Canada,
I try to improve my handwriting,
I hope to help the poor,
I am a smart boy who is religious.

Jeevan Singh (9)
Colston's Lower School

I Am

I am a crazy boy who loves monkeys,
I wonder if monkeys can swim,
I hear the monkeys swing,
I see their habitat going,
I want monkeys to be saved,
I am a crazy boy who loves monkeys.

I pretend that I am a monkey,
I feel that I could fly,
I touch the end of the solar system,
I worry that monkeys will go,
I cry that this human race will go,
I am a crazy boy who loves monkeys.

I understand that we have to go,
I say that nothing is impossible,
I dream that the world is hotter,
I try to be better,
I hope that bad will go,
I am a crazy boy who loves monkeys.

Zak Bond (10)
Colston's Lower School

Blue And White Day

The sand is like the burning sun.
The sea is a blue whale.
The waves are white horses *crashing* on the sand.
The blue sky is the sea.
Boats bobbing up and down like flying fish.
Children building sandcastles on the sandy beach.
White vanilla ice cream is the colour of the waves.
The sea waves are fast like a leopard rushing on the sand.

Lottie Davies (10)
Colston's Lower School

I Am

I am a thoughtful boy who likes football
I wonder what it will be like in the future
I hear the football crowd in my ears as I dream
I see Michael Owen scoring the winning goal
I want to be king of England.

I pretend that I am Michael Owen
I feel that I am boss
I touch the grass
I worry about Liverpool being relegated
I cry when I am hurt
I am a thoughtful boy who likes football.

I understand I must be good
I say football is the best
I dream that I play for England
I try to behave well
I hope to be an astronaut
I am a thoughtful boy who likes football.

James Laver (10)
Colston's Lower School

Blue And White Day

Blue sky and white clouds,
Giant blue waves are crashing white horses,
Seagulls hovering around and round,
White and blue tiny fishes bobbing under the seas,
White fluffy seals swimming in the sea,
Hot boiling sand, giant sandcastles and cold ice creams,
Mmmmmmmm!

Jack Collins (9)
Colston's Lower School

Astray At The Bay

Rocks shimmering in the night,
Birds singing alone at night,
Sand shining,
Waves humming,
Fish swimming, all terrified,
Because they know the shark's alive.

Dolphins swimming joyfully,
All sorts of fish swimming beautifully,
Boats sinking,
People thinking,
People night-swimming happily,
They all think it's a fantasy.

People leaving,
New beginning,
Moon softly moving down,
And the sun is rising.

Cameron Walker-Shepherd (10)
Colston's Lower School

I Am

I am a sporting boy who likes football
I wonder if there is a goalie that scored
I hear the roar of the crowd,
I see myself soaring,
I want to be a football player,
I am a sporting boy who likes football,
I pretend I am a football star.

I feel glad when we win,
I touch the ball with my boots,
I worry that I'll get injured,
I cry inside when we lose,
I am a sporting boy who likes football,
I understand that football should be fun,
I say, 'Let me play!'
I dream about scoring a winning goal,
I try to play fair,
I hope we win,
I am a sporting boy who likes football!

Hamish FitzHenry (10)
Colston's Lower School

Why Do You Have To Die Quickly?

Great plains of rainforest
Your soul is dying quickly
For us human beings
Are the cause of this great shame

The wildlife is kept inside you
As it has done for years and years
Century after century
But still they have lived in harmony with your beauty

I am sorry for your destruction
But it still goes on and on
Just for timber and hardwood
While you are in pain and agony as the rainforest destruction continues.

Hamish Rosser (10)
Colston's Lower School

TREES

T here are many trees in the world today:
H orse chestnut and yew
E lms and willows

R owan and beech to name but a few;
A sh and acers
I ndian bean and cedar
N ettle trees, palms and more:
F ir trees and poplar
O ak trees and lime
R edwoods and maple
E lder and pine
S o many of these trees will not be here
T o brighten the world in eighty years . . .

Sacha Roe (10)
Colston's Lower School

THERE WAS A YOUNG MAN

There was a young man.
He loved to buy soaps and smelly things.
One day he saw stuff he couldn't resist
And the label said:
'If you wash in this stuff
It will stop you smelling like a toad.
Girls will want to go out with you
And they'll chase you down the road.'
The man bought some and used it -
It seemed a really good buy,
But rather than girls chasing him
Many animals had a try!

Thomas Bastin (10)
Colston's Lower School

The Sound Of The Rainforest

Huge colour-mass in the tropics,
Forest, I heard you
Screaming.

Tall trees weeping for the animals,
Crying for the soil, I know
What your dying would do:

Hardwood for our visitors,
Meat for our stomachs.

Falling colour-mass in the tropics,
Trees, I heard you
Whistling.

Soil-low notes, slipping, crumbling:
In the middle of a huge harp
Like a twittering.

We would make you
Bare.

In the hugeness of the forest
Leaves, I heard you
Humming.

Humming to the birds,
You'll never stay there.
Instead of life we choose:

Hardwood for our visitors,
Meat for our stomachs.

Kristian Joslin (10)
Colston's Lower School

The Wild Ones

Don't be fooled by the sea
As it slips in and out of the rocks
Like a cat stretching her paw
And gently turning onto her back.

Don't be fooled by the sea
As it brushes across hot, golden sand
Like the cat who's purring
And flexing her sharp claws.

Don't be fooled by the sea
As it gently breaks on the rocks
Like a cat who's yawning
But is ready to pounce.

Don't be lulled into a false sense of security
For the sea is a moody beast.
It can turn on you just like a cat can:
Both demand respect.

The waves angrily throw about
A lost boat on a stormy sea
Just like the cat as it tosses
And menaces a helpless mouse.

The power they command!
The sea and the cat,
The boat and mouse at their mercy.
They are like kings, the wild ones!

Alison Burbridge-Key (10)
Colston's Girls' School

All Hours

The sky is like a glittery curtain
Draped around the Earth.
The stars are diamonds
Sparkling around the moon, a shiny ball.
All is silent
Still in the darkness,
Nothing can break it
Except the dawn . . .

The dawn comes
Creeping like a mouse.
As the world brightens
Birds sing like angels,
The sky glows gloriously
And the sun rises high in the sky.
The world is beautiful
But time moves on . . .

The dusk is here
Settling on the world,
Pushing it into dark shadows.
It's getting quiet
And the wind is as cold as ice.
Everyone hurries indoors,
Sleepy children are going to bed
Night is approaching . . .

Janine Jones (10)
Colston's Girls' School

The Garden

You open the gate,
And what do you see?
Grass
Bushes
And a great oak tree
With robins
And blackbirds flying around
And the neighbour's cat lying on the ground.
Open the gate
And what do you see?
The sun going down and the frogs a-jumping
With the wind getting stronger
The trees are bumping.
A garden is a place for pleasure and fun
Where all things happen under the sun.

Bella Smith (10)
Colston's Girls' School

My Conscience Is My Rider

My conscience is my rider,
Guiding me through the leafy forest of life,
As each year passes,
A leaf will fade and drop,
Leaving only the skeleton
Which stays to keep alive the memories.

My conscience is my jockey:
After the long ride of the passing years
We see a bright light
And ascend into paradise.

Catherine Clarke (10)
Colston's Girls' School

Lucky Cat

The lucky cat is black as liquorice.
The lucky cat likes to hide and pounce.
The lucky cat has a knack to jump.
The lucky cat has nine consecutive lives.
He will never let a dog attack him.
The lucky cat runs so fast he seems to hover.
The lucky cat will never lack energy.
The lucky cat glides in and out without you knowing.
The lucky cat can slip through the smallest crack like a key
through its lock.
The lucky cat never gets caught by even the cleverest of humans!
Because although the lucky cat is liquorice-black, he can
camouflage himself.
Since the lucky cat is my kinda cat, cute, cuddly and always ignores *13!*

Catherine Stewart (10)
Colston's Girls' School

Sugar

Sugar is a nasty thing,
It rots your teeth and tongue,
It fills your mouth with layers of plaque,
Holes and fillings, a whole stack of that.
Parents tell you, 'Don't eat that!
It rots your mouth and turns teeth black.'
So next time when you take a bit,
Shove it in your mouth and swallow it,
Remind yourself it could raise a spot;
So stop the habit! Stop the rot!

Emily Ebers (10)
Colston's Girls' School

THE WAVES

waves like cannibals
The are hungry

to on small feet.
Waiting pounce a child's

They wriggle, they rush
They make a big fuss
While they're whooshing and waiting to jump.

waves cruel claws
The have sharp

to but they
Invisible us when come

Splash!

quite they caressing feet.
Then suddenly change, your
ready make next

Subsiding to the move.

Karimah Reid-Bailey (10)
Colston's Girls' School

THE EARTH

The Earth is a special,
Spectacular place. It's brilliant,
Fantastic, got only one face. The
Seas are splendid, the weather wild,
The summer's warm, long and mild.
Oceans and seas hold mysteries. Still
Mountains and forests untouched
And free. Our animals are precious;

More species we find, but not all are
Caring, careful and kind. Volcanoes
Are fearsome, bubbling and hot.
So don't spoil our world:
It's the only one we've
Got!

Genevieve Emery (11)
Colston's Girls' School

HUNGRY HORSES

(Dedicated to my pony Dave)

Beanie, Bengie, Barney and Blane,
Eko, Sandy, all hungry again.
Tummies rumble like a lion's roar,
Listening for the creak of the feed room door.

It's open! The horses go mad at the sound,
Neighing and scraping their feet on the ground.
Rainbow-coloured buckets line up on the floor,
Holding the horses' feeds. Some eat rather more!

Like carrots and apples, sugarbeet and swede,
All go to make a tasty tea.
The buckets put in as quick as a flash,
The horses dive in with a clatter and crash.

The food disappears in a flash, like lightning,
The speed it goes down is really frightening.
The buckets are collected and tidied away,
And now the horses quietly munch on their hay.

Lucy Beard (10)
Colston's Girls' School

I'D RATHER BE . . .

I'd rather be a robin than a pigeon,
I'd rather be in a cell than in a dungeon.

I'd rather be a cow than a crow,
I'd rather be fast than slow.

I'd rather be a lion than a cat,
I'd rather be thin instead of fat.

I'd rather be a cheetah than a snail,
I'd rather succeed than fail.

I'd rather be a gorilla than a monkey,
I'd rather be a pony than a donkey.

I'd rather have one head than two,
I'd rather have a cold than flu.

I'd rather be a pop star than in a band,
I'd rather sit instead of stand.

But I'm not any of these; I'm myself
And I'd rather be myself than anything else!

Abioseh Harding (11)
Colston's Girls' School

THE HUNT

I galloped faster than light,
My eyes brown and bright.
A horn sound shot through the sky,
Through the sky it would fly.
Huge wild hedges loomed ahead,
My rider felt like a ton of lead.

Over the hedge I leapt free,
Heart racing within me.
I caught sight of a rusty smudge,
Saw it look terrified, couldn't budge.
I turned away and sped straight home,
Back to the warmth of my stable dome.

Rosalind McClelland (10)
Colston's Girls' School

GOING TO THE SEASIDE

Going to the seaside,
It's cold, sunny and windy,
Going to the seaside,
With my best friend Cindy.

Going to the seaside,
Let's have an ice lolly,
Going to the seaside,
It's better than playing with Polly.

Going to the seaside,
Let's get our spades,
Going to the seaside,
Let's not play charades.

Going to the seaside,
Let's go play in the sea,
Going to the seaside,
Let's go home for tea!

Nicola Price (10)
Colston's Girls' School

Can You Guess What I Am?

This animal moves as fast as sight;
Its eyes are gleaming in the night.
Do you dare to come near?
Approach without fear?
Its claws are sharp, as quick as a dart;
Its tail's like a whip as it thrashes with a flip;
It has soft, short brown hair,
But needs so much care.
Can you guess what I am?

Imogen Napper (10)
Colston's Girls' School

Magpies

Sitting in their nests
Looking rather pretty,
But all their thoughts are filled
With what they could be nicking.

Dressed in black and white
Stealing from their neighbours,
Like spies undercover
Taking things like flavour.

Keeping one eye open
For shining, sparkling gems,
To collect and save forever
Their searching never ends.

Maisie Chilcott (11)
Colston's Girls' School

MY FRIENDS

M y friends are like me, they like the things I do,
Y et they look so different, we dress different too.

F riends are always there in times good and bad,
R egardless of the things I say which sometimes make them mad,
I n fact they help me all the time as only good friends do,
E very friend I have is fun and friendly too,
N ever nasty or unkind are my friends to me,
D espite what other people say, they help me make it through the day,
S pecial friends are hard to find, I like mine because they are kind.

Jade Maslen-Elliott (11)
Colston's Girls' School

OWED TO EARTH

Earth teach me to hold back my emotions,
Like the river tries not to flood.

Earth teach me to smile,
Despite the circumstances.

Earth teach me stillness,
Like the tree trunk is hard to move.

Earth teach me not to rush,
Like a butterfly moving swiftly on air.

Earth teach me to speak my own word,
To not be a sheep but a shepherd.

Ella Massey (10)
Colston's Girls' School

It Kills

It's waiting for something,
It's waiting in the bush,
It's getting impatient,
Its time is being pushed,
Its eyes can see something,
It's now very clear,
It's time for death,
It's going to pounce,
It's getting ready now,
It's out of the bush,
It's got the prey between its claws,
It's getting ripped to shreds,
It's not alive, it's very much dead,
It's something's dinner,
It's walking back to the bush now,
It's ready now,
It's going to strike again,
It's going to cause death again and again,
It's such a cruel thing, as dirty as a rat,
It's a nasty thing, but as fast as a cat,
Its pupils are as wide as lily pads,
It's a rough thing which is as strong as an ox,
It's a mean thing, it's as cunning as a fox,
It's something that leaves us scared,
It's something that we will never see,
It's waiting below the bush, but which one?
It's going to strike again,
It's going to kill,
It's nothing that you've heard of,
It's, gosh, what's that I hear?

It's right in front of you, run, hurry, hurry,
It's too fast for you, it's got to the floor,
It's ripping you to shreds like it's done to something before,
It's killed a weak, helpless thing once more.

Emily Griffin (10)
Colston's Girls' School

Things From The Underground

When nobody's around,
Things come up from the underground.
Scary and mean,
Roaring like a big machine.

Eyes like fire,
But some like coal.
They all have a desire
To rule the underworld.

It's hot (and scary),
It's a monster's paradise.
They've got my friend Mary
And she's crawling with lice!

When nobody's around,
Things come up from the underground.
Not scary or mean,
They're just a scream!

Charlotte Lavin (10)
Colston's Girls' School

Colours

Blue is the colour of the sky,
Brown is the colour of mud,
Yellow is the colour of the sun,
Green is the colour of trees swiftly moving,
Black is the colour of the dark,
Gold is the colour of a shiny golden coin,
Red is the colour of blood,
Orange is the colour of fire,
Pale is the colour of skin,
Silver is the colour of the stars,
Pink is the colour of a juicy raspberry.

Sabrina Alime (11)
Colston's Girls' School

My Dogs

My dogs are always barking and crying
It gets on my nerves, so I put my shoes on,
I take them outside and give them a run,
They get in a mess,
Oh, it's great fun!
I carry them in and give them a bath,
They smell like a treat,
Then we all fall asleep.

Georgina House (10)
Colston's Girls' School

Parents

Without any parents where would we be?
We'd be sitting on the streets and be begging for money,
We'd be looking in the mirror with a gun to our head,
We'd have no food and not get fed.

They annoy me at times,
But that's not a crime,
I'm glad I have parents,
'Cause they're all mine!

Natalia Perepelova (10)
Colston's Girls' School

Benj

M y horse is
Y ellow and beige, he eats

H ay all day,
O ut in the yard he
R uns and plays.
S hying at birds, mice and
E agles.

B enj the beautiful is his name.
E legant walk and marvellous mane.
N aughty at times but I love him all the same.

Louise Rich (11)
Colston's Girls' School

My Dog To Be!

My dog is going to be a black Labrador,
With his tail always in the air.
He'll hopefully be cute,
And is already special to me.
He will only be a puppy,
So very small indeed.
I hope he will be very nice,
'Cause I will be to him.
His name should be Jet,
And every day and every night do I think of him.
He is in my heart,
And will always be in my life!

Kirstie Brown (9)
Courtney Primary School

Pop Stars

Pop stars are glamorous
Pop stars are cool
Pop stars are raving
Pop stars rule.

Pop stars are pretty
Pop stars are nice
Pop stars are wicked
And perform on nights.

Pop stars rock
Pop stars are good
Pop stars are people
That don't live in your neighbourhood!

Robyn Cottle (10)
Courtney Primary School

TURTLE TUESDAY

One day I went to school
I saw something cool
A little green something was in the hall
Its feet were moving, it was kicking a ball!
I went closer to the thing
Then it started to sing
Then it went ping!
It started to spin and went through the ceiling
Then when I saw it, it gave me a strange feeling
As the thing spun past it cut me
Then all of a sudden my knee started healing
Then my orange in my lunch box started peeling
What a weird turtle Tuesday!

Fiona Jones (9)
Courtney Primary School

MY DRAGON

My dragon is small
And isn't very tall.
He also likes to draw.
He really wants to be tall
He can sit on a stool because he's so small.
His name is Charley
He loves fruit and barley
He has a sister called Carly
She's very snarly.
In the morning he brings me the post
In the morning he has toast
For lunch he has roast
And I love him the most.

Carl Challenger (9)
Courtney Primary School

My Sexy Valentine In School

Today I sent my valentine
To a person who I fancy
I told him not to rip it up
So he didn't, he read it
I kept grinning like a Cheshire cat
And put my hands over my head
I was totally embarrassed
And my friends told me well done

So I blew him a kiss
And hoped to see him at lunch
I was waiting for a long time
But time just didn't hurry up
I asked to go to the loo
But I was so excited
I gave myself a mighty grin
Just thinking about what I did!

Carly Hardwell (9)
Courtney Primary School

The Monster In The Attic

There is a monster in the attic
he makes a terrible noise.
Every time I go to bed
he takes me by surprise.
He drinks all the water
out of my glass
and then does a massive, huge, great burp!

Thomas Hooper (9)
Courtney Primary School

My Dragon

My dragon is small
And isn't very tall
He also likes to draw
He really wants to be tall
He can sit on a stool
Because he is small
His name is Charlie
He loves fruit and barley
He has a sister called Carly
She's really snarly
He has small feet
But he still eats meat
When people are frightened
He's delighted
When he ate Uncle Ben
He also roasted a hen
Then sat on a den so
Don't mess with my dragon!

Josh Rees-Smith (9)
Courtney Primary School

My Little Dragon

My little dragon lives at the church,
all day long he sits on his perch
and he toasts my bread
with his mouth flaming red.

His teeth are as blunt as human teeth
and he steals things because he's a thief.
Loves stealing sweets so that his teeth rot
and now he has so many in a pot!

Luke Salim (11)
Courtney Primary School

My Dragon

My dragon is small
and isn't very tall,
he loves to draw
and wants to be tall,
he can sit on a stool
because he is small,
his name is Charlie
and he likes fruit and barley,
for breakfast he had toast,
for lunch he had roast,
he has small feet
and likes to eat meat,
now my dragon poem is complete!

Ben Rudman (9)
Courtney Primary School

UFO

I am a UFO
But I don't say so!
My name is Bobo!
But I still don't say so!
I like to call myself Dodo!
Some people say it's strange!
Would you say so?
I have a secret spaceship
I don't tell though
I am a UFO
'You don't say so!'

Thomas Elliott (9)
Courtney Primary School

Rainbow Colours

Red is the colour of happiness and love,
A sweet bird's song from a heavenly dove.
Orange is the colour of the golden sands,
Falls past your fingertips and runs from your hands.
Yellow is the colour of the burning sun,
A day of hotness has begun.
Green is the colour of the growing grass,
Fields and fields full, a big green mass.
Blue is the colour of an endless sea,
Splashing waves all over me.
Indigo is the colour of the early midnight sky,
Passing stars sailing way up high.
Violet is the colour of lavender smelling sweet,
Other flowers, roses, poppies in a straight line so neat.

Fiona Clabon (11)
Courtney Primary School

1, 2, 3 Poem

One wicked witch had a stitch
Two tabby cats run and jump to catch some rats
Three untamed toys beat up boys
Four newts nibble on decaying roots
Five freaky friends said, 'Depends' to cousin Ben
Six sticky stamps sent to summer camp
Seven stupid shapes play with their mates
Eight enormous elephants squash small pheasants
Nine eggs in a pan, just enough for a growing man
Ten teachers take tales from bad boy beaters.

Jordan Hayes-Collier (10)
Courtney Primary School

What Teachers Do After School

What teachers do after school
Is really quite easy to know
You follow them home one night
And make sure they don't know
They normally go down to the pub
And drink a barrel of beer
Then wander around like zombies
And drink all the beer in the pub
By now they're feeling quite drunk
Then they go back to school
And do all the class' work
They then go back home
And sing a little song in the shower
Then go to bed, snoring by the hour!

Natalie Jefferies (9)
Courtney Primary School

The Monster Under The Bed

When I go to bed
I feel a horrible dread.
I lay there peering around
And stay there hearing the same sound
Of the spooky thing under the bed
And I've always heard what he said,
'Hello Timmy, yum, yum, yum!
I heard you're tasty, yum, yum, yum.'
When I hear it under the bed
I always grab hold of my ted . . .

Gary Coles (10)
Courtney Primary School

When I Was . . .

When I was one I had two thumbs.
When I was two I got on the loo.
When I was three I had a thrill.
When I was four I wanted more, more, more.
When I was five I was alive.
When I was six I loved pick 'n' mix.
When I was seven I believed in Heaven.
When I was eight I was always late.
When I was nine I always felt fine.
When I was ten I had a pen.
When I was eleven I went to Devon.
When I was twelve, at me my mum always yelled!

Amy Harris (10)
Courtney Primary School

My Pet Tyrannosaurus

I've got a pet tyrannosaurus,
His name is Mr Meateater.
He has purple, scaly skin,
Big, round, brown and scary eyes.
Mr Meateater has a pink fluffy girlfriend named
Miss Ladylike.
He lives in a massive rainforest in Indonesia.
Mr Meateater writes to me 12 times a year.
He eats anything he can find such as hairy mice or fat elephants.

I love my pet.

Robyn Scrase (9)
Courtney Primary School

My Magic Box

(Based on 'Magic Box' by Kit Wright)

In my magic box
I will put . . .
Creatures from afar,
Funny jokes that have never been told,
A lamp to wish for whatever I want!

In my magic box
There would be . . .
A crystal from the seven seas,
Treasure from an antique uncle,
Gifts from a prince!

My magic box would be . . .
Covered in pearls and silk,
Padded with linen,
Covered in stars,
From lands afar.

And that is my magic box!

Sophie Gallant (11)
Courtney Primary School

The Animal Rhyme

One cat ate a hat
two dogs sat on logs
three rabbits had horrible habits
four funky flies had to die
five fishy frogs really hated dogs
six silly slugs slithering in some mugs
seven floating fish sat on a dish
eight smelly snakes had some dates!

Ashara Rosser (9)
Courtney Primary School

The Stupid Man

There was a man
Who acted dumb,
He had a pimple
On his bum,
And on his head
There was no hair,
He always swore
He didn't care!

On his knee
There was a scab,
For once he drove
A taxi cab,
He drove it back
Into a tree,
Which fell into
The deep blue sea!

Rebecca McLaughlin (11)
Courtney Primary School

Grandad

My grandad is very big,
He loves trying to dig.
He's strong, brave and bold,
And he is very old.

His favourite sport is football,
His second favourite is pool.
Even though he's getting old,
He still plays sport in the cold.

Scott Owen (10)
Courtney Primary School

Colours

What is black?
St Nick's sack is black,
Slung on his back.

What is grey?
My road is grey,
When I go out to play.

What is white?
The clouds are white,
When it's nice and bright.

What is blue?
My uniform is blue,
But my sleeve isn't because
It's covered in glue.

What is red?
My toy dog is,
Sat on my comfy bed.

What is green?
A hill is green,
In a summer scene.

What is pink?
A pig is pink,
Be careful, they stink.

Steffie Manning (9)
Courtney Primary School

WHAT SHALL I BE WHEN I GROW UP?

What shall I be when I grow up?
Shall I be a newsagent
Or shall I be a glamorous travel agent?

What shall I be when I grow up?
Oh I don't know, oh I don't know,
Oh I am so fed up.

Shall I be a caring vet
Or shall I fly a jumbo jet?

Oh I don't know what to be
When I grow up.

Shall I be an intelligent teacher
Or shall I be a Christian preacher?

Oh I don't know, oh I don't know.

Shall I be a comedian
Or shall I be a person who looks after my friend's chameleon?

Oh I've got an idea actually,
No I don't want to be a plumber.

What shall I be when I grow up?
Oh I don't know, oh I don't know.

I know! I've got the best idea,
I really, really know it this time.
I will just be me!

Samantha Cryer (9)
Courtney Primary School

The Magic Box

(Based on 'Magic Box' by Kit Wright)

I will put in the box . . .
a fire burning, ruby-red,
a dragon sleeping with a heavy head,
a black horse galloping across the moor,
and peace and harmony,
instead of war.

I will play in the box
till the sun goes down,
I'll always smile,
never frown,
while I sit on my dragon,
and think and pray,
that tomorrow will bring
a sunny day.

April Davey (11)
Courtney Primary School

Class Nine

C lass nine are cool.
L ots of loud children.
A nother thing we do is apparatus.
S piders hang silently from our ceiling.
S ilently the class walk in.

N ine is our number.
I am in this.
N obody knows I am writing this
E xcept my teacher!

Jason Gleed (10)
Courtney Primary School

Roller Coaster Ride

R oller coaster speeding fast
O n the track till it's past,
L ong time till it's the end,
L ong, straight line, then a bend,
E verlasting coaster ride,
R ound and round they go.

C ones fall off ice cream 'n' then say no,
O h no, there's a crack.
A argh! They scream, speeding down the track,
S o they pray, coming nearer,
T ill the coaster stops just in time,
E veryone's ever so pleased to be alive,
R oller coaster never rode again.

R iding away in a torrent of screams
I n our creative mind,
D on't be scared to find
E ventually you'll wake up and find it's one of your dreams.

Paige Frere (11)
Courtney Primary School

Sammy Snake

Silly Sammy Snake sat on a silly see-saw.
Silly Sammy Snake played with a silly ball.
Silly Sammy Snake thought it was cool.
Silly Sammy Snake was such a fool.

Silly Sammy Snake made a paper chain.
Silly Sammy Snake was such a pain.
Silly Sammy Snake has done it all again
So silly Sammy Snake had a backache.

Thomas Bignell (10)
Courtney Primary School

CHINESE DRAGON

You suddenly find yourself in China,
Not knowing what to do.
A humongous, fiery-red Chinese dragon appears
From out of the ground.
It is looking hungry, it is going to eat you!
But from out of nowhere a sword and a shield are in your arms.
The dragon looks at you with those big, fierce eyes,
And your legs carry you into a farm.
You run into the farmer's house for safety.
The dragon, he finds you there.
He thinks you're really tasty.

Chloe Scott (10)
Courtney Primary School

THE FAT ELEPHANT

The fat elephant is big and lumpy,
And his stomach is fat and bumpy.
He can't even walk a mile,
He can't put on a smile.

The fat elephant lays down all day,
He can't even stand and stay.
His body is nothing but fat,
His friend is a little black cat.

His tusks are barely sharp,
No stronger than a harp.
His feet are weaker than a feather,
His body is as rough as a leather.

James Metti (11)
Courtney Primary School

Easter

Easter's nearly here,
Chocolate eggs and bunnies,
Shops are nowhere near clear,
Full of bunnies and eggs.

Hip, hip, hooray, it's
Easter today!

Families and friends to buy for,
Spending all our money,
So many eggs to choose from,
Deciding which one to buy.

Hip, hip, hooray, it's
Easter today!

Kerrie Sheppard (10)
Courtney Primary School

My Pets

My pet dog, she likes the fog,
she also loves to run,
me and my dog play in the fog,
it's always so much fun!

My pet cat is really fat,
but he always loves to play,
we can't let him out of sight,
in case he runs away.

My pet rat is really fat,
he eats anything he sees,
but my pet rat is always sat
thinking, *can you let me out now please?*

Jade Gregory (10)
Courtney Primary School

THE NONSENSE DAY

The sky was green and the grass was blue.
The girl climbed up the clock when the mouse went to school.
The ducks began to purr as the cat began to swim.
The pig started flying as the seagull grunted.
The farmer began to gallop when the horse went for a walk.
The sheep made milk as the cow bleated.
What a nonsense day!

Oliver Harman (10)
Courtney Primary School

THE TOMCAT

Tomcat's eyes are flooded with tears,
With his pointy, black, bitten ears.

Teeth like razor-sharp knives
And whiskers like pointy fries.

Mouth like battered and bitten nails,
Paws that feel like crunched up snails.

Tom's tummy rumbles like thunder
His tail's like a python snake's scales.

Lily-May Bennett (11) & Toni Belton (11)
Courtney Primary School

HULLABALOO!

Can you hear the hullabaloo?
It's coming from my magical zoo
The colourful monkeys
And stripy blue donkeys
All jabbered a song to the moon!

Can you hear the hullabamingo?
It's coming from that purple flamingo
The dotty green tiger
And fluffy pink spider
All yelling a song to the sun!

Justin Leflaive (10)
Courtney Primary School

SUMMER

In summer on the beach
With all the sand stuck to my feet,
In summer on the beach
I wonder what people I might meet.

I might meet the flower lady swimming in the sea,
I might meet the vet having a cup of tea,
I might meet the ice cream man serving out his lollies,
I might meet Emma walking over to Molly's,
Who will I meet?

In summer on the beach
With silver sandals on my feet.
In summer on the beach
I met my friend Pete.

We went and had a pizza,
We swam the seven seas,
We went for a walk
And got stung by lots of bees.

After this I had a peach
All in the summer on the beach.

Zara Harris (9)
Courtney Primary School

My Little Dragon

My little dragon
is a funny coloured bird
he comes to my house
and looks quite absurd

He goes to school all day
to learn and to play
then he comes home and
lies on the hay

He reminds me of Adrienne
in a great mood
and he loves
to eat all my food

In the morning
around my room
he flies quietly
like a witch on a broom!

Amy-Catherine Ford (11)
Courtney Primary School

Granny Is A Soldier

Granny is a soldier
big, brave and tough
she can blow people over
with one enormous puff.

She really is a giant
she's as big as a boulder
oh she is really quiet
but still the best ever soldier.

She sometimes goes away
in tanks, planes or boats
to hide from the enemies
they have to wear camouflage coats.

Because now she's getting old
I'm really getting sad
the weather out there is getting cold
but think of all the good times she's had.

George Hobbs (10)
Courtney Primary School

Magic Box

(Based on 'Magic Box' by Kit Wright)

I will put in the box . . .
A flickering firework
A special secret
A thousand twinkling tiny stars
And a dazzling diamond dancing.

I will put in my box . . .
A comfy cushion gazing at me
A red armchair grabbing me in
And a little puppy crying in the wind.

My box is decorated in blue and purple
With flowers all around and then
When you open it the box will shine a light.

I will put in the box . . .
A silver star
A beautiful flower
A gold ring
And a gentle song.

Samantha Derrett (10)
Crockerne CE Primary School

Happiness

Happiness is a gleaming blue going across the Atlantic ocean when
the sun's going down.
It tastes like a fantastic fudge cake with hundreds and thousands on.
It smells like a blow of fresh air when you first wake up in the morning.
It looks like a beam gleaming across the whole Atlantic ocean.
It sounds like a tree swinging up and down gently.
It feels like a soft, fresh pillow when you first lay your head down.

Sam Rugman (8)
Crockerne CE Primary School

Happiness

Happiness is the colour of a kind heart on a Christmas night.
It tastes like a sweet chocolate Easter egg with a gleaming wrapper.
It smells like beautiful fresh flowers just been planted in Heaven.
It looks like a happy spirit floating through the air with a
huge grin on his face.
It sounds like people laughing at a clown throwing pies at people.
It feels like snowflakes falling on your face on Christmas Eve.

Connor Bryant (8)
Crockerne CE Primary School

The School Playground

The rusty bench jumping up and down with a child on it,
Two gloomy toilets flushing on their own,
An old smelly gutter saying horrid words,
The clumsy climbing frame trying to stagger.

The dirty red bin throwing all the rubbish out,
Two whining doors yawning boldly,
Some huge steps were sobbing,
The wild wicked windows were winding people up!

Samantha Dixey (10)
Crockerne CE Primary School

HAPPINESS

Happiness is the colour of red and orange flying through the sky!
It tastes like every flavour ice cream flowing through your mouth!
It smells like fire in the fire guard, ready to warm up.
It looks like a sunset mixed with red on the west side of the country!
It sounds like comedians with a crowd laughing their heads off!
It feels like a cuddly bear that's coming to hug you!

Edward McDade (8)
Crockerne CE Primary School

THE PLAYGROUND

The gutter groans as the wind batters it up.
The drain gurgling as water rushes down them.
TV aerials shiver as electricity buzzes through them.

Great silver poles stand to attention.
Climbing frames try to rip themselves free of the ground.
The chimney coughs as smoke comes puffing out.

Leaves move silently to try and avoid being stepped on.
The benches squeal as people sit on them.
The flag muttering as the wind blows it vigorously.

Thomas Arnall (9)
Crockerne CE Primary School

The School Bell

Waiting for the school bell to ring,
Praying for that metal to do the slightest thing.
Hoping for that tune of hope,
Struggling through class, can I cope?

The minute hand struck ten,
Loosening my grip, I dropped my pen.
'Come on,' I said, as I stood up,
Mr Hewitt stood and knocked his tea cup.

'Harry, what are you doing?' he said,
All the trouble I was in, I wish I'd stayed in bed.
I said, 'Waiting for the school bell to ring,
Please Sir, make it do the slightest thing.'

Harry Sharp (10)
Crockerne CE Primary School

Poem From Pill

A poem pill is a thrill
I met a dog called Bill
He lived on a hill
The owner loved poetry
He is in the military
His dog from Pill is very ill
It is a diabetic
I'm sorry if my rhymes don't thrill
But they are quite poetic.

Gemma Wyatt (9)
Crockerne CE Primary School

WITHOUT ME YOU WOULDN'T BE . . .

Without me you wouldn't be alive,
I gave you food and drink to survive,
I made you see that without me you wouldn't be.

Without me you wouldn't be in the cruise,
I gave you clothes and shoes,
I made you see that without me you wouldn't be.

Without me you wouldn't read or write,
I provided you with gas and light,
I made you see that without me you wouldn't be.

Without me you wouldn't be loved,
I gave you my soul and heart,
I made you see that without me you wouldn't be.

Without me you wouldn't be able to speak,
I knew that you loved to eat leek,
I made you see that without me you wouldn't be.

Without me you wouldn't be so lucky,
I trained you up like a puppy,
I made you see that without me you wouldn't be.

Without me you wouldn't have an education,
I gave you population,
I made you see that without me you wouldn't be.

Without me you wouldn't have a home,
I gave you warmth and made you not alone,
I made you see that without me you wouldn't be.

Adele Taylor (10)
Crockerne CE Primary School

The Magic Box
(Based on 'Magic Box' by Kit Wright)

I will put in my box . . .
A soft, silky, slow snowflake
A brown boat bobbing on water
A little llama looking at a log

I will put in my box . . .

A small bag whistling
A chair eating chocolate
A wall spitting at you

I will put in my box . . .

Rudolph on a sleigh
Santa in a car
A mirror in a window

My box is designed from puppy fur wood
And its fingers are wolves' finger joints
With a hole in the middle for secrets.

Philippa Tremble (9)
Crockerne CE Primary School

Sunrise

Bitter cold.
Little crystal towers standing on the leaves.
Frosty magic.
The frost glistened in the sun.
Freezing cold runs through the mist.
Unconscious hands.
Jack Frost is here.

Thomas Holden (10)
Gillingstool Primary School

A Snowy Day

The magical, sparkling frost coating the ground
Grass is lost underneath, waiting to be found
Footprints marked in the thin snow
All wishing for this day to go
Temperatures of below zero chill people to the bone
Making them want to return to their nice, warm home
The ice crystals gather closely on a single blade of grass
Everyone hoping this day will pass

The large, fat snowflakes flutter through the air
Some making their homes in people's hair
Most of the adults don't seem to see
Just how much fun the snow can be
So the children all go out instead
In their big, bright wellies, shiny red
Only the children want to have fun
The adults just want the day to be done.

Thomas Costin (10)
Gillingstool Primary School

A Frosty Day

Ice is as clear as water
Slippery ice paths
As cold as ice
Sparkly ice
Frosted trees
The ice preserves the plants
The ground crunches under my feet
Oops! I slipped on the ice.

Sam Pinnock (10)
Gillingstool Primary School

A Frosty Morning

Frost!
Bitter cold
Smooth, slippery ice
Collapsed, fainted hands
Clear blue icicles hanging from the naked trees
The ground glimmers, shimmers and glints like crystals
Fluffy ice laid on the bottle-green grass
Frost!

Stephanie Nutman (10)
Gillingstool Primary School

The Peaceful Sparrow

As it glides through the air,
It is leaving peace everywhere,
As it glides past the people,
It makes a wonderful chirping noise,
As people see them in their gardens,
They think, *what a lovely bird that sparrow is.*

Lewis Daly (10)
Gillingstool Primary School

Ice!

Cold, damp ice
Slippery, slidy ice
Sparkling, shiny ice
Crystal clear ice
Ice is chilly
Ice is as blue as water
Ice!

Kyle Reid (9)
Gillingstool Primary School

A Frozen Night

Shivering toes tingle
Frozen
Unconscious fingers
As the morning sun rose the long green grass was frozen
Fluffy, frozen ice laid on the green grass like cold pipe cleaners.
Frost!

Mia Greenwood (9)
Gillingstool Primary School

A Frosty Day

Bitter cold.
Unconscious hands.
Sad, hungry robins.
Twinkling icicles hung from roof tops
As the wind blows past.
Frost!

Adam Turner (10)
Gillingstool Primary School

A Bitter Cold Day

Black ice is frozen
While the bitter wind is blowing
Bitter cold
Icicles hang from the frozen tree
A carpet of ice lay on the floor
Bitter cold.

Ryan Gardiner (9)
Gillingstool Primary School

WINDY WEATHER

Winter is a lovely time
Snow falls like an invading crime
Snow is as white as milk
Holly is as soft as silk
A blanket of snow lay on the ground
It sparkles, it's cold but it doesn't make a sound
Everyone plays and has fun
They throw snowballs until snow's done
Trees stand still and all alone
They stand as still as a stone
Mist hangs thick in the sky
Winter's going, let's say goodbye!

Danielle Moore (10)
Gillingstool Primary School

GOOFY'S LIFE

Goofy has goofy teeth
Because he always eats beef
Sometimes he has a laugh
After he has a bath
He's got a friend called Mickey
A friend called Minnie too
They laugh and tell jokes
With other folks
Like Donald and Daffy and Daisy
He loves Miss Pinkee Pie
He always says 'hi' and 'bye'
But she hates him
She thinks he's dim
And that is Goofy's life!

Jade Smith (10)
Gillingstool Primary School

Storm

The storm bolts across the sky
    Travelling far and wide
        Floating in the dark night sky

As little children weep
    The storm grows near
        But this time it's full of anger
          Clapping and banging

Making people feel lots of fear
    Letting out a wicked cackle
        It's over, the people let out a cheer
          As the sky clears.

Ryan Hurley (11)
Gillingstool Primary School

Sandy Seaside

Tall palm trees sway,
Children shout and play.
The chilly blue sea,
Come and play with me.
Splish, splash,
Wish, wash,
Come and play with me.
Up on the pier,
The time is near.
Hearing children laugh,
Posh people pass.
I'm not going home,
So leave me alone!

Sally Cave (10)
Gillingstool Primary School

Forest Fire

A lightning bolt shoots across the sky,
People say, 'Look at that fly!'
It hits the forest and makes a flame,
But how do we know who's to blame?
The forest gave off a huge big spark,
Burning off all of the bark.

It's burning, it's burning.

The flames are burning orange and red,
While some of us still are asleep in our bed.
The firefighters rushed quickly to the scene,
And tried to put it out with a water beam.
It was so very hard to put it out,
So the green goddesses came within a shout.
With all that water power,
It was out within an hour.

It's out, it's out.

Rob Olive (11)
Gillingstool Primary School

Frost!

Freezing feet,
Red noses,
Unconscious hands.
A huge blanket of snow
Covers the ground.
The soil crunches under
Each footstep.
It's as cold as ice!

Charmaine Gray (10)
Gillingstool Primary School

Seasons

Spring, sun comes up from behind the hills
Spring, melting away all the snow
Spring, daisics pop up from the ground,
Spring, and the sun as bright as can go

Summer, the sun burns the back of your neck
Summer, everyone is out to play
Summer, melting away your ice lolly
Summer, everyone wants it to stay

Autumn, leaves falling off the trees
Autumn, it gets really dark
Autumn, it gets much colder
Autumn, and all that is left on the trees is bark

Winter, snow laying on the ground
Winter, as white and soft as can be
Winter, making people laugh and shout
Winter, covering all the trees.

Rachel Dors (10)
Gillingstool Primary School

A Wintry Place

Bright cloudy skies
The bitter blustery blow of the wind
A carpet of snow covered the green grass
Crystal ice towers in groups of many
Ice catching the light
Frost on one side of the branch
Wrap up warm for
Winter is here!

Aidan Peppin (9)
Gillingstool Primary School

A Frosty Winter's Day

Fresh, thick, freezing snow
Bitterly cold
The cold, chilly blow of the wind
The carpeted snow lay as white as the pages of a new book
Icicles hang from the forest trees
Cold ice
The snow is here
Jack Frost is near.

Daniel John Fennell (9)
Gillingstool Primary School

Terrible Teachers

Teachers are clever
Some teachers are bright
When the headmaster starts to shout
They get in a fright
Blah, blah, blah, is all they do
Don't they go to the loo?
Finally the day ends
The teachers go, 'Hooray!'

Christian Holden (10)
Gillingstool Primary School

Surprising Spring

After winter, spring will come,
Then the bees will start to hum!
Flowers will open their little eyes,
They will be in for a big surprise!

Lambs jumping, skipping too,
Cows will start to *moo!*
Trees will open their flowers,
And you will smell their powers!

Hannah Walker (10)
Gillingstool Primary School

AUTUMN

Leaves drop from the sky,
Making not a sound.
All around colourful leaves cover the ground.
Trees stand tall in the cold weather.
People drop things like feathers.
Night falls,
Squirrels gather their nuts and go to bed.
Next morning will come,
Everyone will have good fun.

Laura Wright (11)
Gillingstool Primary School

THE STORM CAT

S eeking its prey,
T he storm cat has started,
O rganising its approach,
R aging through the water,
M ouse hole watch out,

C laws digging, paws pawing,
A t last he's got through,
T oo late, he's got you.

Ryan Kent (9)
Gillingstool Primary School

The Storm Cat

Howls of thunder,
Fur of raindrops,
Eyes of lightning,
Claws of dark clouds.
That is the storm cat.

Scraping at the windows,
Ripping at the walls,
Roaring over the breakwater,
Growling at the boats.
This is the storm cat.

Pouncing at the waves,
Leaping over rocks and hills,
Now the storm cat has gone to sleep,
We're safe until next winter.

Rhys Coghlan (8)
Gillingstool Primary School

Shivering Snow

Snow is soft, gentle and white
Don't stay out too long,
You might get frostbite.

Snow is fresh and icy cold
Don't go out if you're bald!

Snow covers fallen leaves
Don't walk out with ice creams.

Snow helps to forget
Don't get too wet.

Joe Boyd (11)
Gillingstool Primary School

The Storm Cat

The storm cat pounced and bounced towards its prey,
It sprinted and printed its paws on the muddy, damp grass,
It snarled and scratched as it crept closer to the steep hills,
It thundered from the sky.
As the storm cat got nearer to the woods,
It howled at the creatures through the trees,
It tried to grab its prey, but its prey was much too fast,
It scratched on the barks of trees,
It pounced angrily around the woods,
And it howled like a werewolf.

Racheal Birt (8)
Gillingstool Primary School

Storm Cat

The sneaky cat cries in the distance,
The wind's getting
Louder and louder,
Crashing, bashing,
Getting faster,
The storm is coming.

The wind is howling like a wolf on a mountain,
The storm cat is scratching at people's windows,
Howling, growling,
Getting closer,
The storm cat is here.

Nicola Hurley (8)
Gillingstool Primary School

The Storm Cat

The storm kitten stirred as she woke from her sleep,
She sniffed everywhere, looking all around.
She grew into a storm cat and started to snarl,
The storm cat leapt onto the hills and howled.

She grabbed the roof of the mousehole as she tried to get in,
She scratched at the windows of the houses.
She cried as she hunted for her victims,
Her cry echoed like roaring of thunder.

Shanelle Facey (9)
Gillingstool Primary School

The Storm Cat

The storm cat hunted the boats
Like the boats were mice,
As it pawed its way through the waves.
Its paw leapt with fear,
As it tried to get into the harbour.
As it approached, people ran, fearing it.
The storm cat hunted for food,
As it got closer, it growled louder . . .

Joshua Pring (8)
Gillingstool Primary School

The Storm Cat

The storm cat sniffed
As it pounced up high,
It pawed at the boats
As if they were mice.

The howl of the thunder
Crashed and the storm cat
Grabbed its prey.
The storm cat roared
In the wild wind.

Charlotte Caise (9)
Gillingstool Primary School

THE STORM CAT

The storm cat peeks with frightening, gloomy eyes,
It crawls behind houses,
It must be the storm cat,
The storm cat scratches the windows,
It covers the dark rocks,
It must be the storm cat,
The storm cat is really fierce,
It never comes out in tears,
It must be the storm cat,
It must be the storm cat.

Jessica Watt (8)
Gillingstool Primary School

A WINTER DAY

Fresh, thick snow covers my frozen feet,
I get up in the morning - everything is white.
Fluffy ice lies on the grass like pipe cleaners,
Cold toes tingle,
The icicles are as clear as water,
Winter.

Kaylyn Jefferies (10)
Gillingstool Primary School

A Frosty Day

As I walk down the icy path,
I see sparkly ice hanging from the trees,
The ground is like diamonds and jewels,
Shiny crystal towers are reflecting on the leaves below,
The snow glistens in the light of the moon,
As the morning sun rises, the grass freezes,
Jack Frost must be here!

Chloe May Taylor (10)
Gillingstool Primary School

The Storm Cat

The rain was dripping down from the sky,
The storm was crying, high and high.
The storm cat scratched against the windows.
The storm cat is now here,
He's already got you,
He's digging, he's scratching,
He's got through.

Cheryl Nutman (8)
Gillingstool Primary School

Frosty Feet

Frosty feet freeze in the freezing wind,
Foraging foxes forage through the fierce winds,
Icy faces melt in the chilly wind.
Squirrels scrabble over stones in the winter wind,
The winter snow drifts in with a chill,
The deepening snow shines in the winter sun.

Jacob Moore (9)
Gillingstool Primary School

The Cold Ice

Winter,
The crunchy leaves scattered on the slippery ice,
The green grass is frozen like fluffy pipe cleaners,
It's bitterly cold,
Cold as ice,
The ground sparkles like diamonds,
The glittery ground shines like moonlight,
Ice as clear as water,
Winter!

Claira Vizard (9)
Gillingstool Primary School

Snow

S is for snow, soft and silver crisp,
glittering in the dark.
N is for numb fingers in the cold,
O is for an open field,
where everybody plays.
W is for winter's snow - glistening
crystals falling on the ground.

Jasmine Hardie (8)
Gillingstool Primary School

Snow

Snow is glittery, crispy and frosty
Snow shows our footprints and hand prints
Snow is stiff, soft and white
Snow is slippery, cold and icy
Snow is crystal icicles.

Megan Morgan (8)
Gillingstool Primary School

A Snowy Play Time

Snow is crisp and crunchy on a winter's day,
Now is the time to play.
Snowmen are kicked down.
Drifts of snow in a pile.
Snow is fantastic in the playground.
Snow is crystals all around.
Snow is fun-tastic!

Connor Palmer (7)
Gillingstool Primary School

A Winter's Morning

A winter's morning is full of fun!
Robins singing one by one,
Singing joyfully, they lift their heads;
The wind is biting their little legs.
I go downstairs: the garden is white,
The leaves are crunchy,
The snow is bright.

Henry Carter (8)
Gillingstool Primary School

Frosty Days

Bitter cold,
Unconscious hands,
Temperatures plummeting down,
Sparkly ice,
Freezing feet,
Slippery paths,
Winter!

Lewis Stone (9)
Gillingstool Primary School

Frosty Icicles

The morning sun rose, the grass was frozen,
The bitter wind blew.
Shiny crystal towers glistened above the leaves,
Crystal clear.
Crystals lay twinkling on the ground,
People's unconscious hands,
Black ice across the freezing lanes,
Temperatures plummeting down.

Victoria Holden (10)
Gillingstool Primary School

A Snow Poem

Snow is slippery, it is fun
Snow is fun; you can throw
        snowballs at people.
Snow is icy icicles
        hanging from trees.
Snow is crispy on the ground.

Danny Llewellyn (8)
Gillingstool Primary School

Snow

Snow is soft and cold,
It looks shiny not dull.
We can make snowmen
And have fun in the sparkling,
Lovely snow.
I love fresh, crispy snow.

Charlie Max Freeman (8)
Gillingstool Primary School

Winter Snow

Snow is children playing with snowballs
And building snowmen
Snow is white and crystal clear
Snow is fun and joy
Snow is slippery and hard
Snow is laughing and shouting
Snow makes tingly fingers
Snow is frosty leaves.

Lauren Ayling (7)
Gillingstool Primary School

A Winter Poem

W ellies for the slippery snow,
I cicles so spiky.
N umb, tingly, freezing fingers,
T rees are white and frosty,
E xploding, shooting snowballs,
R unning children, beaming faces.

Oliver Carter (8)
Gillingstool Primary School

Snow

One early morning
The snow was falling
Snowflakes were shining crystal clear
I heard my friends laughing
Screeching and throwing snowballs
Everywhere was happy with beaming faces.

Lisa Derrick (7)
Gillingstool Primary School

Snow

I like snow, playing in it is fun.
The snow is white and glistening,
crystals shine in the sunlight.
I make prints with my hands and feet.
Pretty patterns stuck onto the snow.
Snowflakes falling from the clouds
into a tree covered with snow.

Jessica Gordon (8)
Gillingstool Primary School

A Snow Poem

Snow is cold, it makes my feet tingle.
Snow is icy, soft and glittery.
Snow is frosty.
Snowflakes spin in the air,
they pop and fizz.
Snow is crunchy.
We can make snowballs.

Shannon Miles (7)
Gillingstool Primary School

A Snow Poem

Snow is soft,
As soft as a feather mattress.
Outside I hear robins sing,
I see my footsteps in the snow.
I feel happy and excited.
Snow makes my fingers cold and tingly.
Snow is shimmery and such a lovely sight.

Paige Haughton (8)
Gillingstool Primary School

FROSTY

Bitter cold,
Unconscious hands,
Sparkly ice,
The ground shines like diamonds,
Sliding feet across the ground,
Shiny, crystal towers shine above the leaves.
Crystal clear,
Shivering leaves.
Frost!

Emily Cox (9)
Gillingstool Primary School

SNOW

Snow glistens in the sparkling sun.
Snow is crunchy and crispy.
Snowflakes fall on the rough, rocky ground.
Bitter winds bite the flowers and the grass.
Snow is like little crystals in the ground.

Kelsey Reid (7)
Gillingstool Primary School

SNOW

Snow is crystal clear, crispy and cold
Snow is snowflakes falling from the sky
Snow is fun, excitement, bright and white
Snow is building snowmen

Snow is throwing snowballs at each other, playing games
Snow is running, skidding and sliding
Snow is shouting, laughing and screeching
Snow is beaming, joyful faces.

Lauren Tuck (8)
Gillingstool Primary School

The Healthy Daisy And The Dying Dandelion

(In the style of Blake's paired poems)

The Healthy Daisy

Oh healthy daisy how I see
The way you sit and bloom for me
Although you sit behind the tree
You give me sunshine and lots of glee.

But when a cloud comes into sight
It always gives you a huge fright
But I was born to help you fight
So overhead I fly my kite.

The Dying Dandelion

Oh drooping dying dandelion
Do you hear me speak?
Just sit there doing nothing
I know that you are weak.

Oh little dying dandelion
I think it's time for you to go
So to you I say goodbye
Although I love you so.

Daniel Ager (11)
Mangotsfield CE Primary School

Where Do All The Teachers Go?

I pursued home a teacher
Right across the park
She began playing football
Until it was quite dark

She trotted home wearily
Her heels made a noise
I'd never heard before
It sounded more like a tortoise

She reached her tiny cottage
And opened up the gate
She turned around and glared at me
It was an awful fate

I stared for a moment
I had a huge surprise
Her face had no crinkles
And she had awfully pink eyes.

Ross Britton (10)
Mangotsfield CE Primary School

Fog

Gradually the fog comes up behind me
Seeking and searching
Playing tricks on me
Hedges disappear
The fog weaves in and out of my fingers
Seeking like a blind mole searching
He traps people and then they fade.

Sean Keld (10)
Mangotsfield CE Primary School

WHERE DO ALL THE TEACHERS GO?

Where do all the teachers go
When it's four o'clock?
Do they live in houses?
Do they wash their socks?

I followed one home today
And this is what I saw
He took off his head
And much, much more.

He disappeared out of the room
I had a great big shock
As he entered
I saw the king of pop.

Elvis Presley stood there
I thought that he was dead
But there he was in front of me
'The king is here!' he said.

Jim Wale (11)
Mangotsfield CE Primary School

SUMMER

On a summer's day birds fly
In the clear blue sky,
People eat ice creams at the seaside
Hey, here comes a tide
Bees are flying in the sky
So is a butterfly
The sun is shining on this Earth
Some people like to surf.

Rosie Pearson (10)
Overndale School

CHRISTMAS POEM

Christmas is here
It only comes once a year
Christmas lunch all around
Under the tree presents can be found

For lunch we will have turkey
At tea we'll sit under the tree
Crackers go off with a bang
Christmas stockings we will hang

Sleigh bells will ring
Christmas carols we will sing
Christmas games we will play
'Ho, ho, ho,' Santa will say.

Georgina Daniell (9)
Overndale School

MY CAT LUCKY

My cat is black,
He likes to attack.

Lucky is my cat,
He sleeps on the mat.

He likes to play with me
And share my tea.

Lucky is very fat,
He likes to catch a rat.

My cat has a wet nose,
He plays with the hose.

Emma Ridley (9)
Overndale School

CHRISTMAS POEM

Christmas is coming
Elves are busy
My family is humming
And very dizzy

Robins are red
Trees are in the shop
I'm asleep in my bed
Crackers go pop

We're doing a Christmas play
Costumes are made
People will have to pay
To watch it this day

We are giving a cheer
Rudolph is having a carrot
Santa's drinking a pint of beer
I want a parrot!

Francesca Causon (8)
Overndale School

JUBILEE

The Queen has reigned for fifty years
It's time for us to give her cheers.

We're partying for Jubilee
Everyone's happy, even me.

We all want to play in every way
To celebrate this special day.

Declan Mulhall (10)
Overndale School

PET POEM

My pony is called Maisie
She is all black
Maisie is good at jumping
When it is raining I put on her mac.

Maisie is soft and cuddly
She is like my teddy bear
Maisie is very stubborn
She is a silly mare.

My pony is sweet
But sometimes silly
She thinks she's got a friend
I would call her Tilly.

In the summer
She plays with her friends in the field
But in the stable
Her bucket I will mend.

Maisie is spoilt and lucky
She's got a rug, bucket and hay net
What else could she have
She is a wonderful pet!

Eleanor Luffman (10)
Overndale School

SUMMER

In summer the sun comes out
Birds and people are about
Butterflies here and there
Bumblebees everywhere.

At the seaside I will play
I wish I could stay all day
In summer the trees all have leaves
I can see very busy bees.

Alexander Harvey (10)
Overndale School

APRIL SHOWERS

April showers
Are happening now
It changes weather
I don't know how.

It's nice and sunny
Now it's raining
I need my umbrella
The sun has come out again.

I'm off to the beach
To have some fun
Now it's cold
Where is the sun?

It's going to rain
I'm running home
When it rains
I always moan.

Here is the sun
Hooray, hooray!
Now I can
Come out to play!

Abigail Britton (10)
Overndale School

Pet Poem

Campo is the best
Better than all the rest
He sleeps on your head
When you are in bed

Eric is a cat
He is quite big and fat
Eric climbs on walls
And loves to play with balls

Spike has had three different collars
He plays with dollars
Spike is always ill
He takes a pill

Boris is cute
He sleeps in a boot
He has a red nose
Which looks like a rose

Guy is very shy
He could not hurt a fly
He has a skinny tail
His claws are as sharp as nails.

Megan Mulhall (9)
Overndale School

Autumn Poem

The leaves are falling off the trees
Now it is autumn there is a lot of breeze
In autumn it rains quite a bit
But sometimes we are lucky and it only spits

Sometimes in autumn it is sunny
But you'll very rarely see a bunny
The leaves are turning yellow, brown and red
Now they are that colour you know they are dead.

Charlotte Causon (10)
Overndale School

PET POEMS

I have a hen called Ermintrude
She is red and brown
When I give her lots of food
My mum begins to frown.

George is a lovely cat
He is black and white
He likes to sleep on a mat
And wakes up with a fright.

Charlotte Dimond (9)
Overndale School

AUTUMN POEM

Hedgehog is bed-making,
Ready for his sleep
Robin sits quietly
Stop to take a peep
Leaves fall off the trees
Leaves fall off because of the breeze.

Lawrence Luffman (7)
Overndale School

HALLOWE'EN POEM

Devils are red,
They never go to bed.
The witch's cat
Is on her hat.

Witches are here,
I want to cheer.
Ghosts and Dracula are in the sky
Flying very high.

Vampires are here,
I don't want to cheer.
Pumpkins are bright,
They glow in the night.

Kerry-Dee Shaw (7)
Overndale School

AUTUMN

Autumn is here
The leaves fall off the trees
The branches appear
Oh dear, autumn is here.

It's windy in autumn
The leaves are all blowing
To the ground
They are all going!

Sally Page (10)
Overndale School

AUTUMN POEM

Autumn is here
And all is clear
Every leaf that falls
Makes the trees seem tall

Autumn is a nice time of year
I cut the hedge with the shears
When the leaves have turned brown
They fall down to the ground.

Louis Walker (10)
Overndale School

MY FRIEND BEN

My dog is lazy
He hides in the daisies
My dog is black
He runs on the mat

He likes to play
In the hay
My dog is small
He climbs up the wall

He doesn't like the cat
So he sleeps on the mat.

Charles Porter (9)
Overndale School

What A World

Rotten, deadly, toxic fumes rising like fire into the air
Poison, poison, polystyrene boxes
Disintegrate, intoxicating the air
Sticky, oily sea carrying death for sea creatures
Reflections from shattered glass on the seabed like a smashed,
cracked mirror
Litter floating up and down on the waves
Waves squidging on the rocks, oily blobs float on the sand
Nice, little streets filled with rubbish chucked on the clean ground
Lots of people polluting the air not taking care
Chopping trees down just for cheap food
Millions of pieces of rubbish bobbing up and down on the clear sea
Earth should be peaceful, peaceful like people care.

Annie Harris (8)
St George CE Primary School, Queens Parade

What A Sea

Smelly oil chucked in the sea
Oily waves squidging against the rocks
Waves splashing against the stones
Whales having a heart attack
It makes us sick
It makes us feel
Angry
Sad
Cross
We don't want it to be like this ever again
If there wasn't any pollution in the world it would be great
A clean world would be cool.

Adam Day (8)
St George CE Primary School, Queens Parade

WHAT A WORLD!

Toxic waves of gas rising in the air like fire
Oil spreading along the waves like it's taking over the sea
Waves of litter smashing the rocks
Black fumes in the air like the world is on fire
Stop poisoning the fresh air and it will be a better place for young and old
Think of yourselves as well
The land and the sea will be fresh and healthy for young and old
The forest will be full of animals
People will be healthy
Children will be delighted playing games
Let the world live on.

Alexander Smith (7)
St George CE Primary School, Queens Parade

WHAT A WORLD!

Animals all over the world are in danger.
Birds stuck in sticky oil far from flight.
Oil squiggles on the waves.
Deadly gas rises like fire.
Broken glass sitting on the seabed.
Fish choking, dying in oil.
Never throw rubbish on floors.
Did you throw your rubbish away?
Pollute the planet, we will die.
Save it, we will live.
We will stay safe.

Joshua Hale (8)
St George CE Primary School, Queens Parade

Toxic Gases

Deadly, toxic gases rising like fire into the air
Poisonous, poisonous polystyrene boxes
Disintegrate, intoxicating the air
Sticky, oily sea carrying death for sea creatures
Reflections from broken, shattered glass on the sea bed
Like a smashed, cracked mirror
Litter floating up and down on the waves
Waves squidging on the rocks -
Oily blobs flop on the sand.

Seals being hauled onto the shore swamped in blobby oil
Little starfish stuck because the oil is so sticky
But . . . it doesn't have to be like that
Put your rubbish in the bin, you can stop wasting -
Say no to pollution.

If you do put your rubbish in the bin, imagine what it would be like:
Flowers on every street corner,
Animals being able to swim freely -
Without being covered in oil.

Joseph Marche (9)
St George CE Primary School, Queens Parade

Elephant

E lephants are big and grey
L ike buses, only bigger.
E lephants eat anything
P lants, vegetables and buns.
H ave you ever seen an elephant
A nd wondered what she's called?
N elly is her first name.
T hat's all!

Christopher Day (7)
St Ursula's High School, Westbury on Trym

The Harbour

The gulls swooped in as the public were eating their
Cornish pasties.
They pecked up the crumbs with their sharp yellow beaks
and flew away to the rooftops of the town.
The fisherman gutted his fish as the gulls came in
for another snack.

The harbour cat prowled around and snatched the fish heads
from the old, salty nets.
It was hard to believe that the ancient rusty fishing rods
would catch a fish.
Then there was a loud scream as a barefoot toddler
stepped on a rusty hook.

Jonathan Partridge (10)
St Ursula's High School, Westbury on Trym

Follow Me

'Follow me,' he said.
'Come to a cliff edge, so near,
Stay with me -
Don't leave!'

So she followed . . . !

She danced in his arms all night,
Not aware of the closeness of the cliff edge.
But then, she did not come back at all.

They found her on the beach below,
She'd followed - she just had to go!

She was on every news' front page
And all because she'd followed him!

Alice Bushell (10)
St Ursula's High School, Westbury on Trym

The Zoo

It's boiling hot at the zoo,
The heat is driving the animals *cuckoo.*
The tiger is on the brink -
The visitors are just running for a drink!

Everyone's trying to keep so cool
Apart from the sea lions – they have their pool!

The heat is driving everyone mad;
The monkeys' behaviour is very, very bad.
Everyone's looking for some shade,
The gorillas are under a shelter which they've made.

Everyone's trying to keep so cool
Apart from the sea lions - they have their pool!

The visitors are queuing for ices all day long,
The monkeys are howling a very strange song.
The lion is ready for its feast
And roaring like an angry beast!

Everyone's trying to keep so cool
Apart from the sea lions, they have their pool!

Haydn Linsley (9)
St Ursula's High School, Westbury on Trym

My Cat Fluffy

My cat Fluffy
has black and brown fur.
She is as fluffy as a rug and
when she's sleeping, she never makes a stir.
Her hair is always knotted
and looks untidy.
But you never know what
she might be hiding!

She lies on the floor
waiting by the door
for me to come into the house.
She likes to nibble my toes,
then off she goes
to search for a playful mouse.

Lauren Weetch (7)
St Ursula's High School, Westbury on Trym

THE COVE ON THE COAST

Waves running up the beach
Wind blowing my hair and biting at my cheeks.

In the sea, we moor our boat
And in the sea, it floats.

Half pebbles - half sand
Whilst up on the cliff, a stretch of forest land.

The sea wrestles the ragged rocks;
It pounces on the sand, like an angry fox.

Once we found a dead whale,
Which was as long as the beach (including the tail).
Whale Beach is now the new name!

Whale beach is where we come
To have a picnic in the sun.

There are lots of wild life in the bay,
It's my favourite place to play.

It's my favourite place to play
On the rocky coast of Devon.

Lucie Cast (9)
St Ursula's High School, Westbury on Trym

A Lion's Life In The Zoo

Lions are stared at all day long,
With nothing to do at all;
It's boring for them to have nothing to do
Not being able to catch their own food.

Lions needs to pounce and play
With space to run around
All these lions can do, is sleep all day
And dream of a life, running free.

Lions in zoos should be released into the wild,
Instead of being imprisoned in a zoo;
With nothing to play with -
And nothing to do.

Robby Crees-Luget (10)
St Ursula's High School, Westbury on Trym

A Place I Know!

This place I love, is quiet,
I have not been there since I was three years old.
When I visit the place in my mind
It brings back memories - old memories;
This place is in the Caribbean.

In my head, I see the silver sand,
I feel the gentle breeze, stroking me.
Bright fish swim in crystal seas.

Dolphins diving - whales leaping and crashing;
Their thunderous splashes churning the water -
Turning it into a mega tsunami!

Lauren Grant-Adams (9)
St Ursula's High School, Westbury on Trym

School Poem

I hate school - but have to go
It's a rule!
I have to wake up - oh so early
How awfully annoying!

Oh, I like maths and French
But not that horrible old school bench!

In fact, they are so mean
They won't even let you use the vending machine!

I think that every school should have a pool
To make it much more fun.
A bit of wet play, every day
Would brighten our day at school.

I heard some children bawl the other day
But I suppose they were only small.

Hopefully, one day, we'll all get used to school!

Cecily Jay (10)
St Ursula's High School, Westbury on Trym

Spring Poem

Spring is lambs leaping
Spring is rabbits - hopping playfully.
Spring is birds, singing sweetly
And spring is animals waking up from hibernation.

Spring is flowers popping up;
Spring is grass, bursting through thick layers of snow.
Spring is daffodils - like a yellow carpet
And spring is banks of melting snow.

Georgina Bourne (10)
St Ursula's High School, Westbury on Trym

I Hate Exams

Oh, I *hate* exams
Oh yes I do!
Always having to be silent
And never knowing what to do!

Oh, I absolutely *hate* exams,
They're such a pain.
It's not as if they'll bring you fortune or fame!

Oh no! It's Sunday, the test is on Monday!
And I am really feeling quite sick,
Fractions and decimals, still to learn
And time is passing too quick!

The exam begins -
And I start to sweat.
All the sums I've learned
I start to forget!

My heart's beating faster,
My pulse is sky high.
The stress is killing me -
I'm going to die!

My hand begins to shake
I'm frightened that I will fail.
Will I still make it to college?
I doubt my work will be acknowledged!

Oh, I *love* exams, because I've passed!
Yes, it's time to party!
But wait a minute, what if the others call me *Smarty?*
Aggh, I *hate* exams!

Amy Willerton (10)
St Ursula's High School, Westbury on Trym

COLOURS

Colours are bright
Colours are beautiful
Colour is everywhere!
They are such a wonderful sight.

People have colours
All over them.
Red, yellow, pink and green
All of these colours you can see.

Red lorries, cream tables,
Purple spotted hats.
Green plants, brown houses,
What are we going to do without them?

Colours brighten up our day
So we can have fun and play!

Sunsets are colourful
Blue, purple, red and orange.
You can see why
Colours are so important!

Tino Kuwana (10)
St Ursula's High School, Westbury on Trym

LITTERBUGS

Litterbugs, litterbugs, over here, over there.
Crisp packets over here, over there.
Litterbugs, litterbugs, over here, over there.
Litter bins empty but lots of litter on the ground,
Over there and there and there . . .
Please put your litter in the bin!

Reece Johnson (11)
St Ursula's High School, Westbury on Trym

SPRING

Spring is here, the daffodils are coming out like
Jack-in-the-boxes, and the blossom is decorating the trees
And the lambs are being born.

The nights are getting lighter and the Earth is waking up,
Everyone is happy that spring is here.

Spring, spring is here, let's have fun with each other,
Thank you God for our world!

David Buckland (9)
St Ursula's High School, Westbury on Trym

ACROSTIC POEMS

S ally was slithering on the grass
A lways hissing, always fast.
L ooking all ways, where she went
L ooking for a lovely lunch
Y esterday, she climbed a tree.

S ally snake saw a squirrel
N ext day, she saw a cat.
A t last, the sun began to shine
K illing mice, is always nice.
E at the mice, that's nice!

Jonathan Hulin (7)
St Ursula's High School, Westbury on Trym

SLITHERING SNAKES

Slithering snakes glide around
Little snakes don't make a sound.
Python snakes spat and spit
Big snakes don't need sports kit!

Small snakes slither out of sight
They are hiding quietly, to give you a fright!
There are lots of snakes in the world you see,
I am glad they don't slither by me!

Megan Steven (7)
St Ursula's High School, Westbury on Trym

FOOTBALL

In my life I have a dream to play for a football team.
My favourite club is Man United, van Nistelrooy
and Beckham get me excited.
When I watch them on TV, I think to myself,
that's where I want to be!

For my birthday, my mum put pen to paper,
and received a letter back, ten days later.
On this photo, was number seven!
Yes! You've guessed it! It's David Beckham!

I couldn't believe that he'd found the time to send the photo
which is now mine. I have put this picture in a frame,
hoping it will improve my game.

I like to watch them when I can,
I am a Man United fan!
I'd like to watch them live, to see van Nistelrooy take a dive.
To be in the crowd and see them win.
Oh, what heaven I'd be in!
To witness them in all their glory,
that is now the end of my story.

Ollie Parnell (10)
St Ursula's High School, Westbury on Trym

THE LEOPARD

The leopard prowls at night
be aware, it might give you a fright!

The leopard usually hunts the deer,
be warned, because it will always be near!

The leopard is quick at catching its prey,
and they are very lazy cats, because
they usually sleep in the day.

Leopards are very silent cats,
and they are very domestic cats,
and they wouldn't mind eating a rat!

Leopards have large spots,
they have a lot of spots,
and they usually get hot!

Lucy Coulter (10)
St Ursula's High School, Westbury on Trym

THE DIVER'S STORY

The diver in the sea, can see many wonderful things,
Underneath the sea there are sharks lurking
Who scare you!
Jellyfish, which hurt you and
Angel fish who are beautiful and
Lobsters, which scuttle about.
Whales who amaze you, and coral
That surprises you!
The diver may spend his lifetime
Seeing different sea creatures.

George Sawkins (8)
St Ursula's High School, Westbury on Trym

The Snow

The snow is very soft
The snow is like a white sponge.
I like playing in it
I like making snow angels.

When it snows
I rush out to play in it
To make a snowman
With a funny hat.

The snow means
No more school.
It's too dangerous to travel in the snow
So that means, *no more school!*

But when the winter is through
The snow disappears.
I'll be sad to see it go -
It will come back next year though.

Robin Fisher (11)
St Ursula's High School, Westbury on Trym

Love

Love is great
Love is wonderful
Love is everywhere
Love makes our world go round
Everybody has some love inside them
Even bullies have love inside them.
I love somebody - do you?

Cormac Ferrari-Power (8)
St Ursula's High School, Westbury on Trym

Brown Paper

Brown paper, brown paper
What do you see?
A kitchen, a fire
And a brown cup of tea!

Brown paper, brown paper
What do you think?
I love that brass saucepan,
On the bright kitchen sink!

Brown paper, brown paper
What will you do?
I will live in this drawer
For a month or two!

Zareena Fitchett (11)
St Ursula's High School, Westbury on Trym

The Clumsy Poem

One, two
I'm very clumsy
Three, four
Because I dropped my plate
Five, six
I clear it up
Seven, eight
I ran away
Nine, ten
I do it, over and over again!

Jessica Bookham (10)
Stockwood Green Primary School

How I Feel

I feel happy and full with glee,
I like to write all about me.
I like to chat and gossip all the time,
So that's why I'm writing this rhyme of mine.
I like going to school because I think it's cool.
I like to play in the playground because I can run around.
At home, I always read in my bed
And that's where I put my sleepy head.
When I wake up, I rub my eyes
And if it turns out to be Saturday - that will be a surprise.
Sometimes I play with my brother,
Sometimes I watch my mother.
On Fridays, I go in the tub and after I go down the club,
Then I go to bed and rest my sleepy head.

Lacey Barnaby (7)
Stockwood Green Primary School

Gambia

I went to Gambia on a long haul flight
It took us almost all of the night.
When we arrived. Oh, what a sight!
The sand was so soft and the sea was so hot.
The weather was just right, it stayed warm all night.
I loved the sea, it was a friend indeed.
The birds and the trees were all new to me,
But the alligators and monkeys
Frightened me. Oh how I loved
That beautiful, blue sea.

Saffron Heard (10)
Stockwood Green Primary School

My Grandma's In Stiches

My poor Papi, Grandma's not here,
To feed the sheep his ginger beer.
Nor give to the sheep and lambs
Grandma's famous bread and jam.

My grandma's not been very well
A story here that I must tell.
She rarely goes to see the doctor,
And never moans when something hurts her.

Because of this, we know full well
She really must be going through hell,
When she says she's feeling poorly,
Something must be hurting, surely?

Everybody rallies round
In a crisis, we have found
The Pompiers Annie did call
So glad on the ice they didn't fall.

To the hospital they did hurry,
And other cars they made to scurry.
To Urgencies they took poor Grandma
And tried to ask her to say 'Aaggh!'

If it weren't serious that would be funny,
It wasn't her throat, it was her tummy,
Which made my grandma feel so bad,
And poor Papi to be so sad.

To the theatre she was taken
Which left my Papi rather shaken.
It wasn't a play she went to see,
This was a surgical emergency.

Our mummy wanted to be there,
To sit with Grandma and to stare
She'd never seen her mum in bed
And lots of tears she did shed.

Aunty Ona keeps feeding Papi,
Trying to keep him feeling happy.
Uncle Ian puts the chickens to bed,
'All done!' at night, he's often said.

Uncle Martin and Annie do the baking,
To the market the cakes they're taking.
Everybody tries to do their best
While Grandma has a well-earned rest.

I hope that this silly letter
Helps to make my grandma better.
I want to try and do my bit
Because with Grandma I cannot sit.

We will go to France in the summer,
'I love you Grandma!' I will tell her.
'Sorry I wasn't there when you were ill
But Mummy said I must go to school!'

Hayley Clements (10)
Stockwood Green Primary School

Cakes

Pancakes
Sugar cakes
Crunchy cakes
Cakes are yum
Because they
Fill up your tum!

Paris Lynes (8)
Stockwood Green Primary School

Our Holiday Poem

The poem we're about to write
Is all about our holiday on the Isle of Wight.
We all jumped into our big, green car
When we got there, our mum opened a jar.
She said, 'Sit down, we're having toast.'
Then our dad shouted, 'I'm having the most!'
After that, our dad burped and said, 'Excuse me!'
We stepped outside and saw the sea
So we decided we'd go to the beach.
When we arrived, our mum gave us an ice cream each
We went home to our tent
And by us, there was a house for rent.
We went to the swimming pool
To play some volleyball.
At the beginning, there was the toss,
In the end, we lost!
We jumped back into our big, green car
Then our dad pulled out his big, brown guitar
And he sang 'Humpty, Dumpty, sat on a wall'.
When we got home, we sat in the hall.
Now we've explained about the Isle of Wight
Now you know, we're truly right!
Who knows, we might go there another day?
And that was our summer holiday!

Ben Francombe (11) & Adam Francombe (8)
Stockwood Green Primary School

Bums

Big bums,
    Little bums,
Fat bums,
    Small bums,
Chubby bums,
    Skinny bums,

Spotty bums,
    Wrinkly bums,
Soft bums,
    Bony bums,
But most of all,
    I like my *bum!*

Laura Jones (9)
Stockwood Green Primary School

THE CRASHY SEA

Sea. What a sight!
Crash! What a fright!
Swiftly as her waves go by.

She tastes salty and fishy,
Sandy and gritty.
Watching her fish go by.

She can be rough by thinking she's tough,
You'd think she'd learn her lesson!

She's grey, green, yellow and blue
She feels cold. What about you?

She likes to hide behind her rocks,
She can give you a terrible shock.
So be careful when you go near sea
Because you *don't* know what she will be!

Lizzie Rose (11)
Stockwood Green Primary School

My Family

My dad has a clever mind and is really kind.

My mum does the cleaning, shopping and cooking,
she's really sweet and loves it when I tickle her feet.

My brother Liam is the eldest and he thinks he's the tallest.

Ryan, my brother, is 14 and he acts like 13,
I can't believe that he's not in a football team!
My sister Hannah, is like a big skinny banana.

Then there's me - Emma Carroll,
but my dad calls me - Emma Barroll!

Oh yes, not to forget my cats, Sooty and Sweep,
They're fluffy and always asleep.

Emma Carroll
Stockwood Green Primary School

My Dog

My dog likes to go out and play
He never runs away.
He stays by my side
When we go for a ride -
On a nice hot summer's day.

Ashleigh Brough (9)
Stockwood Green Primary School

Kirsty's Poem

My name is Kirsty, I am six years old
I like to be warm and I hate to be cold
I love my doll's, teddies and toys
And I really like to make a noise.
Sometimes I wear my hair in a pony tail
I have a brother called Gary and a sister called Kel.

Kirsty Cockram
Stockwood Green Primary School

My Bedroom

My bedroom is small
but very tall.
It's full of toys for little boys
and I make a lot of noise.
It's yellow and green and
in it, I have lots of dreams.

Danny Brough (6)
Stockwood Green Primary School

Baby Sisters

Baby sisters cry
Baby sisters pull your hair,
Baby sisters get you told off.
Baby sisters cling round you all day,
But mine is sweet as can be . . .

Okay, my baby sister is a terror!

Lucy Seager (9)
Stockwood Green Primary School

Surprise By Breiz

When I'm at home all alone
I'm feeling very sad
Then my friends call round to play
And I'm really very glad.

Breiz Lynes (7)
Stockwood Green Primary School

Night-Time, Fright Time

Night-time, fright time,
Please leave on the light time

Night-time, dragons slam
Thunder flashes

Night-time. fright time,
Please leave on the light time

Night-time, fright time
Monsters *roar*

Night-time, fright time,
Please leave on the light time

Night-time, fright time,
Fireworks *bang,* trees rustle

Night-time, fright time,
Please leave on the light time

Night-time, fright time
People stamp

Night-time, fright time,
Please leave on the light time!

Shannon-George McKee (7)
The Manor CE Primary School

That Was The Day

That was the day
When the brush started singing,
And the whiteboard began to boogie.

That was the day
When the bed looked bored,
And the tap caught a cold.

That was the day
When the sink started crying,
And the carrot hopped away from the fridge.

That was the day
When the keys flew away
And the flowers watered themselves.

Hazel Jones (9)
The Manor CE Primary School

Pet Poem

One cuddly cat
Two dotty dogs
Three furry fish
Four marching mice
Five happy hamsters
Six rushing rabbits
Seven bluebirds
Eight clucky chickens
Nine slimy snails
Ten hungry horses.

Liberty Nicholls (5)
The Manor CE Primary School

Morning

Morning comes
With next-door neighbours banging.

Morning comes
With Daddy snoring.

Morning comes
With staircase creaking.

Morning comes
With alarm clocks ringing.

Morning comes
With door slamming.

Morning comes
With babies weeping.

Morning comes
With cats miaowing.

Laura Glynn (7)
The Manor CE Primary School

One Old Otter

(Alliteration Poem)

One old otter opening oysters
Two tiny tigers twinkling on tables
Three tiny terrapins talking
Four fabulous fine fish
Five funny fluffy flies.

Steven Day (8)
The Manor CE Primary School

My Colour Poem

I like red
A rose is red
I like blue
A bluebird is blue
I like green
A frog is green
I like yellow
A daffodil is yellow
I like pink
Sunset is pink
I like orange
Tissue paper is orange.

Gemma Aitchison (5)
The Manor CE Primary School

One Old Ordering Octopus

(Alliteration poem)

One old ordering octopus opening oaks,
Two talking turtles touching tigers,
Three thundering tigers tearing turtles,
Four fair flamingos flapping fiercely,
Five fighting flies finding flowers,
Six sad spiders safely spinning,
Seven sliding snakes sliding silky sausages,
Eight elephants eating eggs,
Nine newts nibbling noses,
Ten tall telescopes tracing trees.

Robyn Brailey (8)
The Manor CE Primary School

Morning

Morning comes with raindrops splattering.
Morning comes with doors squeaking.
Morning comes with people snoring.
Morning comes with a car crashing.
Morning comes with people walking.

Conor Follett (6)
The Manor CE Primary School

Excited

Excited is like . . .
Going on holiday with my family
Waking up on Christmas Day
Getting a new baby
Spending time with my friends
Watching Arsenal beat Man United.

Jordan Gale (10)
The Manor CE Primary School

Hidden Treasure

A treasure is not the purest gold that's hidden beneath the sea,
A treasure is not crystals and gems that sparkle like a bright star,
A treasure is not creamy pearls that bring all people riches,
It isn't even fragile china that must not be broken!
This treasure is much more pure than gold and silver bars,
This treasure is a part of you; this treasure is your friends.

Naomi Cassidy (11)
The Tynings CP School

OWNER WANTED

Must be hairy,
Good with sticks,
Thinks it's cruel to teach dogs tricks.

Give long walks,
Muddy races
Mustn't mind a few chewed laces.

Must be playful
Must love puddles
Must love warm and cosy cuddles.

Must know teeth
Need bones to gnaw
Must drop titbits on the floor.

Must be scruffy
Must love meat
And let me have a yummy treat.

Must be bouncy
Mustn't be neat
Must have very smelly feet.

Esther Harrill (10)
The Tynings CP School

IN THIS IMAGE I CAN SEE . . .

Bright sunset gleaming,
Calm water as people sleep,
Dirty horses walking like prowling tigers,
A bridge beaming brightly,
Colourful reflections rippling in the water.

Faye Mason (11)
The Tynings CP School

One Night I Met . . .

One night I met a monster,
He was big, hairy and blue,
I asked him what his name was,
'I don't know,
But here's a clue!'

First he tried to scare me,
But all I did was stare,
He tried to hit me slowly,
But all I did was grab his hair.

One night I met a dog,
Looking for some food,
I let him in my house,
And he was really rude.

He tried to bite me,
All I did was jump,
He tried to scare me,
All I did was give him a thump.

One night I met an alien,
Looking for some Coke,
I poured him a glass,
But all he did was joke.

He tried to trick me,
But it didn't work,
He tried to kick me,
All I did was throw the Coke.

It landed in his face and trickled down his vest
He got very wound up,
He shouted at me
And then he slunk away.

Ryan Johnson (10)
The Tynings CP School

Ute Prayer

Desert please give me caring
As a fennec fox cares for her cubs

Desert please give me blossoming
I smell a scent like a rose

Desert give me freedom
Let me free from your clutches

Desert give me peace
Freedom's all I want

Desert fill my heart with emotions
It has sunk down very low

Desert stop me from suffering
As an elephant is fought for his tusks.

Claudia Jacob (10)
The Tynings CP School

Ute Prayer

Earth teach me stillness
As the rain pours down on me.
Earth teach me suffering
As the tropical birds suffer.
Earth teach me happiness
As the monkeys play happily.
Earth teach me peace
As the trees sleep peacefully.
Earth teach me courage
As the predator approaches me.
Earth teach me to forget myself
As the beautiful Earth dies.

Jordan Walsh (11)
The Tynings CP School

THE HIKER, THE TROLL AND THE SILVER NECKLACE

'Oh amazing Hiker, amazing Hiker, what is your necklace?'

'It is made of pure silk, Troll, why do you stare at it?'

'Give it me.'

'No!'

'Give it me. Give it me.'

'No!'

'Then I will yell at night in the mountains,
Run through the snow and yell for it.'

'Troll, why do you want it so?'

'The silver shines like a sparkling moon,
And glows like a diamond in the sky.
Give it me, give it me soon,
Or I will give a great cry.'

'Shhh, I stole it from the stars.'

'Give me your necklace, I want it.'

'No!'

'I will howl in the day and night for your necklace,
I love it so
Give it me, give it me!'

'No!'

'The letters engraved in sparkling green
Shine like a beautiful sapphire.

Give it me! Give it me!
I love it so!'

'No!'

Aaren Hopkins (9)
The Tynings CP School

Overheard In The Toy Box!

'Woody, Woody, what is your hat?'
'It's pure cotton and made in China.'

'Buzz, why do you like it so?'

'Give it me, give it me!'
'No.'

'Then when you are asleep I will pull your wadding out
I'll snap your pull string and hang you from the ceiling,
Give it me, give it me!'

'No!'

'If you don't, I will scream and shout, tell Andy
that we are real!
Give it me, give it me!'

'No!'

Christopher Wright (10)
The Tynings CP School

School Dinners!

Every day in school,
When we've finished PE,
The clock strikes twelve - it's lunchtime,
If only you could see!

Mangled carrots, cauliflower,
Lumpy custard too,
The pudding's as bad as the main course,
Apple pie in stew!

Guess what happens if you don't eat it all?
You are sent to the rotten head,
He sends you straight back again,
So it's shoved down your throat instead!

Also on the menu,
Are totally burned chips,
If you put them in your mouth,
They will totally burn your lips!

All of my friends,
Think the same as me,
That school dinners are disgusting,
You should come and see!

Rachel Say (10)
The Tynings CP School

The Blind Girl

In this image I can see . . .

People standing whilst the winds blow.
A house standing there with the rainbow staring at the girls.
Light calm grass blowing in the winter wind.
Dark sky closing in.
The river flowing through the grass.

Trees and bushes standing there at an angle.
Metal from the instrument gleaming in shining sun.
The butterfly, lying, having a dreamy rest.
Animals walking, looking and thinking.
Crows crowing in the distance.

Stones sitting, not daring to move a muscle.

Emma Hazlett (11)
The Tynings CP School

UTE PRAYER

Earth gives me stillness
As the rain pours down.
Earth teach me suffering
As wild animals suffer in memory.
Earth teach me humility
As tropical trees are humble with beginning.
Earth teach me caring
As the mothers nurture their young.
Earth teach me courage
As the predator approaches.
Earth teach me limitation
As the snake hisses along the ground.
Earth teach me freedom
As the parrot soars through the sky.
Earth teach me resignation
As the leaves which love the rain.
Earth teach me regeneration
As the baby which grows in the spring.
Earth teach me to forget myself
As the drying rain forgets its life.

Sam Elliott (11)
The Tynings CP School

In This Gloomy Photograph . . .

Dark, reddish sky above orange sky,

Enormous elephants as big as a giraffe with a brownish rock on their back,

Faded orange sun just above the light orange sky,

Dark, dusty mountains just behind the enormous elephants,

Two tiny people playing in their desert, running away from the large elephants.

Rebecca Jones (11)
The Tynings CP School

In This Busy World . . .

Snowy mountains curl like sharp and solid waves.

Sloping hills in a busy, noisy village.

Huge houses creak and scream in the wind.

Barking dogs stroll slowly, looking fearsome.

Bushy brambles covered in snow.

Dull black headscarves covering their heads.

Samantha Wood (10)
The Tynings CP School

UTE PRAYER

Ocean tide give me stillness
As waves crash against the mighty blue whale.

Ocean tide give me movement,
As the seaweed sways across the sand.

Ocean tide teach me calmness
As the unaware stingrays smoothly swim.

Ocean tide give me freedom
As dolphins glide up, down and around the surface.

Ocean waves give me courage
As the birds dive in the cold water.

Elliot Martinez (11)
The Tynings CP School

IN THIS VISION . . .

A swarm of young children crowd the city,

The old-bricked school groans with glee,

The massive flats block out the skyline,

The crimson trees sway back and forth,

The prettily-paved pavement is crushed by people.

School is out!

Oliver Sheppard (10)
The Tynings CP School

UTE PRAYER

Sea teach me happiness
As the clouds are filled with light
Sea teach me calmness
As the waves gently tap against the rocks
Sea teach me peace
As the dolphins soar through the sea
Sea teach me strength
As the great white snatches its prey
Sea teach me anger
As the water slashes against the coral
Sea teach me freedom
As the whales who slide in and out of water
Sea teach me kindness
As the sea horse cares for her young
Sea teach me to shine
As the sun shines through the clouds
Sea teach me to forget myself
As the sand lies on the seabed
Sea teach me luck
As the shell finds an owner
Sea teach me limitation
As a seal, swimming so carefully, watching for its young.

Jade Morch (10)
The Tynings CP School

SCHOOL CUSTARD

School custard is very sick,
School custard is so thick,
Every day it is served in piles.
It is served to children,
For miles and miles!

Gemma Chandler (9)
Weston Park Primary School

FOOTBALL

F ootball is a great sport
O ften I play
O ffside is one of thc rulcs
T raining is hard but fun
B oots have to be worn
A nd shin pads to protect your legs
L ots of people watch the game
L ove football . . . it's great!

F erdinand is great
O wen too
O vermars is quick
T hierry Henry hits the mark
B eckham's number 1, although he wears a 7
A lan Shearer plays for Newcastle
L jumberg's got red hair
L ove Man United!

Rebecca Jenkins (9)
Weston Park Primary School

SNOWING

S now is cold, snow is freezing
N othing feels like it
O ak leaves falling
W alls covered in snow
I like snow - it is in my dreams
N obody's hot because it's cold
G oing out, having fun.

Ewan Estcourt (7)
Weston Park Primary School

A School Acrostic Poem

S ome people love to learn.
C opying down the work silently.
H oping they have passed their tests.
O n the table sit six books.
O n the chairs sit six people.
L istening to the teacher in silence.

Sophie Wheeler (8)
Weston Park Primary School

Animals I Like

I love cats, I love dogs
But I hate bats but not frogs
I like gerbils but they have terrible habits.

I love animals, any animal for you?

Charlotte White (8)
Weston Park Primary School

Bedroom

My bedroom is full of toys
I like to make lots of noise
My friends come over
I don't know why
I like to have lots of fun!

Kelly Hill (9)
Weston Park Primary School

School

S ecretary is in charge
C hildren are good
H ungry children enjoy their lunch
O bey the rules
O pen the doors
L ittle people come to our school!

Alex McGill (8)
Weston Park Primary School

Worms

W iggly worms wiggle around
O n the ground
R ound and round the garden
M y mouth says, 'Pardon!'
S plash, splash, splash!

Amy Hart (9)
Weston Park Primary School

Fears

Freaky at night.
Everyone's going to
Get a fright.
A ghost haunts all night.
The ghosts are out on a
Spooky Hallowe'en night.

Dale Hill (8)
Weston Park Primary School

THE LEOPARD'S DINNER

I see a birdie, a birdie today
Alone in the treetop working away
Alone he might seem but there're others around
People try buying him for only a pound
He's not that good-looking like others may seem
Even though the winds have finally been
Stooping down in the bushes below
A leopard is walking very slow
Finally it makes its stunning attack
Then there's the bird flat in his lap!

Jamie L Hawkins (8)
Weston Park Primary School

MY DREAMLAND

In my dreams
So it seems
Nothing matters
They go from friends to mad hatters
Clouds and pretty kittens
Woolly scarves and fluffy mittens
In my dreams
So it seems
There are suns, moons, stars
As well as multicoloured cars
I love my dreams
So it seems!

Molly Scull (9)
Weston Park Primary School

Hamsters

Hamsters like going in their ball
They run round and round.

Hamsters are great, they sleep all day
And play at night, they hide their food
And sneak around and when they see you
They go to ground.

They hide their food in their pouch
And when you're not looking they empty it out.

They pick and choose what food they eat
And sometimes I give her a special treat.

Kirsty Hannan (7)
Weston Park Primary School

A Poem About Our School

What have you done today?
Every day we try our best
Smile every day
To make you feel proud!
Over the hills
Now what a fun day
Play all day long
Around the playground we play
Run around all day
Kick a ball all day long.

Ceri-Mai Shepherd (8)
Weston Park Primary School

My Dolphin

One dolphin is a special one
He flips, slides and glides
He splashes, crashes up high
He turns around and sees me
He gives me a hug and cries
And then he turns around and says, 'Goodbye.'

Vivyan Jouxson (8)
Weston Park Primary School

Sun

The big red sun is shining
Shining in the sky
I love bathing in the sun
It's shining on my window
I love the sun.

Ashley Govier (8)
Weston Park Primary School

Pets

I've got a puppy
He is so fluffy
He purrs like a cat
And eats like a rat
He gets his face all grubby
His tummy is so fluffy.

Taylor Cunliffe (8)
Weston Park Primary School

Flowers

I love flowers, they make me sing
They make the birds spread their wings
When they start to cut them down
I do a very big frown
Why do people stand on flowers?
But they don't really know they have powers
I love flowers!

Oliver Rush (8)
Weston Park Primary School

Light

Lanterns flashing
Illuminating the skies
Glowing brightly
Hills shining
Tiny stars glow in the night.

Deakon Richards (8)
Weston Park Primary School

Knight

Kills people
Knocks people over
In the dark
The knight in silver armour.

Kurtis Ware (8)
Weston Park Primary School